Google

Classroom

Definitive Guide for Teachers to Learn Everything About Google Classroom and Its Teaching Apps. Tips and Tricks to Improve Lessons' Quality

COLOR EDITION

JEREMY PAGES

Table of Contents

CHAPTER ONE
GOOGLE CLASSROOM

Google Classroom and how it works

Google Classroom is a free online service created by Google to aid as a collaboration tool between students and teachers to ease the exchange of files or documents from one person to another. The main purpose of the Google Classroom is that it is designed to allow for easy creation, sharing and assessment of assignments on the part of the teachers while the students can also answer and submit for grading without the need for printing; the streamlining of this process is done by the Google Classroom. Online classrooms can be created by teachers and then the students are invited, after which assignments and other class activities can follow. The progress of each student can also be tracked on the Google Classroom along with sending emails to the student and their parent. This helps teachers to keep tabs on students and have a real-time feedback as to which of the students have completed their works or not.

Google Classroom integrates your classroom with Google Documents, Google Mail, Google Forms, Google Calendar, Google Sheets and Google Slides into a single platform hence totally avoiding the use of papers. Classes can be joined by either having your students imported from the domain of a school or by invitation through a private code. Google Classroom has the Google Calendar integrated in order to aid with assignments having due dates and also class speakers.

Features of the Google Classroom

Asides from just providing a platform to submit assignments, the Google Classroom also provides further features of grading the assignments, providing comments in the Classroom or communication, report of originality, courses can be archived, and others.

Assignment

The Google Classroom provides the platform that allows for storage and grading of assignments between the students and the teachers or between students and students. The files are prepared on the Drive of students after which it can then be submitted for grading. To avoid a situation where a particular document is viewed, copied or edited by all of the students, teachers can proceed to use a file as a template as this helps each student to have access to their own copy which can then be edited and then graded upon submission. There is also the added feature for students to attach extra documents to their assignments from their Drive.

Grading

There are different ranges of grading schemes on the Google Classroom. Teachers can also have files attached to assignments which are sent to students on an individual basis. Files can be designed by students in a situation where the teacher failed to create the file, after which they can attach the file to their assignment. Each students progress can also be monitored and tracked by the teacher as they, the teachers, have the option to edit and pass comments. To allow for the assignments to be revised, graded assignments are turned back to the students with or without additional comments by the teachers. Graded assignments cannot be edited by the students but only by the teacher.

Communication

Teachers are able to pass announcements to the classroom and in a bid to allow for communication in both ways between the students and the teachers; the students can also make comments under the post. Posts from students can be moderated as it does not have such level of priority as any post from the teacher. Google Drive Files such as documents, sheets, slides and YouTube videos can also be attached to any post in a bid to have such content shared. The Google Mail has an option provided in the Google Classroom interface that allows emails from the teacher to be sent to one students or multiple of them.

Originality Report

This is a recently added feature that helps in improving the writings of students as it has missing citations flagged and also helps to highlight source materials. This is done by helping students, teachers and Google classroom users to identify sections or parts of a work that has been submitted which contains such particular wordings or parts of an alternative source. This also provides teachers with the opportunity to check for the integrity of the assignments submitted by their students. There is however a limit on how you can use the originality report as this depends on the version of Google Classroom you are using.

Archive Course

Courses can be archived in the Google Classroom by teachers at the end of a year. Archiving a course removes it from the class homepage and has it placed in the area for Archived Classes. This is a move to help the teacher maintain organization and orderliness in the current class. Archived courses are however always available to be viewed by the teachers and students although no changes can be made to such courses unless the teacher has it restored.

Mobile Applications

Google classroom app was introduced for the mobile phones few years ago and is now available on both Android and iOS devices. This app allows you to have files shared from other apps, take photos to attach to your assignments, and also enables you to access it while offline.

Privacy

Google classroom does not support for advertisements or the likes. The interface for teachers, students and other users is not scanned and does not show any advertisements.

Why use the Google Classroom?

1. Provides Exposure to e-Learning Platforms

In recent times, it is imperative for students to have participated in any online course while studying for a degree. This is more needed especially if you decide to take a master's degree in education as you will do more work online. Introducing your students to the Google Classroom at such a young age helps to expose them to using the online platform and helps them in the future as the Google Classroom is super- friendly to users.

2. Ease of Accessibility

Google Classroom is easily accessible from any platform on your mobile device or via Google Chrome on your computer. Materials are easily accessible even from the comfort of your room as teachers and students alike have all the files uploaded on Google Drive in a folder 'Classroom'. You can add as many learners as you so desire to your class and there is no difficulty in logging in or receiving or submitting assignments.

3. No presence of paper

There is no need for papers when running the Google Classroom. Once the teacher and student have internet access, they can then handle all of the class works and assignments over the internet. On uploading assessments or assignments to the class, they get automatically saved to the Drive. Also when students have their assessments or assignments done and submitted, it is saved to the Drive. This prevents the issues of printing, handing out or even misplacing your work.

4. Saves Time

Google Classroom is very effective hence it helps to save time. All the materials are saved in one Drive hence the teacher can easily access the Classroom at any time and place and this affords the teacher with time to do other things. Google Classrooms are also accessed from the phones hence students can also multitask while being in class.

5. No Work is Ever Lost

Google Classrooms are always available on the internet and not on your hard drive hence your work saves automatically and can always be accessed from any device connected to the internet. Teachers and students do not have to worry about carrying large chunks of books or hard drives around before they can access their class. Situations like 'I lost my book' or 'My dog destroyed my flash' are avoided as your work is protected on the Drive.

6. Differentiation

It is easy for teachers to have instructions, materials and due dates differentiated while not having anyone singled out. Teachers can decide to send new materials or assignments to individual students or the whole class. To do this, there are just few processes that are taken while having the assignment created on the Classwork page.

7. Effective Feedback System

Providing students with feedbacks is a very integral part of impacting them with knowledge. The feedback system in the Google Classroom is very effective as there is the option to provide support to the students as they are working right away. This helps the students as they can get fresh comments and feedbacks which will definitely have more impact on them than pre- recorded comments.

8. Communication and Engagement

It has been observed and proven that technology helps students to get engaged and also aids communication. Google Classroom provides a platform that eases communication and engagement between the teachers and students. There are tools that also make communicating with the parents easy. Providing opportunities for students to answer questions in the Classroom also helps them more engaged in the classes. Mails can also be sent between the students and the teachers along with streamed posts, private comments and feedbacks on assignments. Teachers can also manage and control posts and comments made by students. Mails can also be exchanged between the teachers and the parents.

9. Track Student Progress

Google Classroom provides the option that allows you to track real- time student progress. The Screen Work screen allows you to monitor the real- time progress of any particular student when you click on any student. Google Docs or Google Slides have the comment feature which helps to show evident feedback. A students productivity (or not) can also be monitored by using the revision history. You can also use the revision history feature to monitor whatever changes must have happened since the last time you viewed.

10. Involves Parents in Student Progress

Google Classroom helps to provide parents or guardians with a overview once in a week of the streams from your classrooms, posts, dates that assignments are due and announcements. This also helps to notify parents in case their child or ward has missed any assignment or assessment as it will be indicated.

How Does Google Classroom Compare To Other Online Classrooms?

As you might be aware, Google Classroom is not the only type of online classroom that is available. We also have the Apple Classroom for the iOS software and the Microsoft Classroom.

The Apple Classroom is a very versatile app that is used to aid learning on the iOS software (the iPad and the MacBook). This app encourages mass sharing and also individual connections as it allows for work to be shared and also helps the teachers to have their students devices managed. It allows you to launch any particular website, app or any page of the textbook on any available iOS device in a class, documents can also be shared between teachers and the students or student to student, and you can even go ahead to have such shared works projected on a monitor or TV using your Apple TV. This helps you to monitor individual students as it shows you the apps they are working on, you can have specific tasks assigned to each individual, have their passwords reset and you can also have their devices muted. At the end of each class, the summary of each student's activity is available for you to view.

The Microsoft Classroom is a platform that has been blended online for learning in schools and its aim is to ease the grading of assignments and ensure stress- free communications between the teachers and the students without including paper. Considering areas that did not have access to the internet, the Microsoft Classroom introduced a feature 'Surface devices'. The Surface device is similar to a tablet however it comes with pencils and other wonderful accessories.

The Google Classroom compares to the other online classrooms in the following ways:

1. Student Friendly Price Tag: It is no longer news that Apple products are more expensive than Google products. This price difference is a good reason why according to recent statistics, most devices in schools use more of the Google Classroom than the Apple Classroom. Also the Google Classroom uses technology that is more compatible with everyday tasks that are related to learning in schools.
2. Sharing: Google Classroom offers a wider range of sharing than other online classrooms. This is as a result of the G- Suite including Google Mail, Google Docs, Google Sheet, Google Slides etc, which are all comprehensive and really important sectors of learning and education. This provides a very efficient platform of learning to every member of the class; including the teachers as it is easier to have their worked managed and coordinated in effective ways.
3. Accessibility: Google Classrooms are designed to be very accessible on a wide range of available devices today. This software strategy has made Google Classrooms a top choice for most educators (teachers and students included), unlike the Apple Classroom which is only accessible from iOS devices (iPad and MacBook).
4. Offline Access: This is a plus for the Microsoft Classroom as they added the Surface device for students placed in geographical areas with no internet. This helps them to still use the classrooms as they have added accessories like pencils and others.
5. Management: The Apple Classroom is a platform majorly to help you have your students devices managed in the classroom while the Google Classroom is a platform not only to coordinate your class but also to manage the whole process of creating assignments, grading them and also its submission.

Implementing Google Classroom in Your Classrooms

In all honesty, you cannot just decide, all of a sudden, to start using the Google Classroom as this will majorly result in a struggle of creating enough time to manage your resources and the devices. In a bid to however advance and have the best experience from the Google Classroom, it is important that you have measures and tools put into place and this should be done at a pace so both teachers and students do not feel rush. Some keys to having Google Classroom introduced to your classroom include:

1. **Have a goal.** You should be sure of what you want to gain from the Google Classroom. You shouldn't plan to involve in this just because fellow teachers or schools are involved. The goal should be one in line with both teacher and students needs. Specify your goal and it is important to attach a timeline so you can plan accordingly.

2. **Plan.** You are familiar with the saying, 'Failure to plan is planning to fail'. The plan should be one that carries along the interest, maintenance, upkeep and training of all teachers, students and also administrative. You should also put measures in place i case problems arise and someone or people should be assigned with such duties.

3. **Choose a Leader.** As you are planning and assigning roles for implementation, it is ideal to have a leader chosen as this helps to keep the plan in check and makes all steps accountable for. This leader could be for a committee or an administrator or even a teacher.

4. **Test- run the plan.** It is ideal for you to test run the idea before it is introduced to everyone. A small group should be formed including the administrative, teachers and students and then they should make use of the Google Classroom before it is brought to the others for use.

5. **Current Technology.** It is necessary to be aware of how much technology you are exposed to in order to confirm if it will be able to support your new goals. Will your current network system be able to support additional computers or devices? It is very important to know this before you embark on such projects so you do not get stranded mid-way.

6. **Be sure to embark on what's ideal for you.** It is necessary for you to know what both the teachers and the students need; hence you can decide what's best for them. You should make proper enquiries before embarking on your idea.

7. **Access at home.** It is imperative that your students should be able to access the Google Classroom anytime and anywhere; hence for students who reside in poor communities without internet, it is necessary to check for programs, both local and national, that can assist such students in order to put the device to effective use.

8. **Ascertain if your idea is succeeding.** From the moment when the idea is conceived up to when you have a plan to every step, you should assess them and make sure you are making progress. You should also check how effective and efficient your measures are turning up to be.

9. **Set Limits.** It is not unusual for students or even teachers to want to misuse access to the internet. This is why limits should be set and also there should be attached consequences for people who default on the rule, as it would not be ideal to just take away the device from them. You might have to put such monitoring software in place so as to be able to manage them.

CHAPTER TWO
BASICS OF GOOGLE CLASSROOM

Creating and Managing your Google Classroom

It is imperative for you to have a Google account before you can use this Google Classroom. Hence if you do not have a Google account, you should go to *gmail.com* to create one. Once you have a Google account, you can then proceed to your Google Classroom.

1. You have to sign in to *classroom.google.com*. You can download the Google Classroom app if you are using an iPhone or Android devices. The app makes it very easy for you to access the Google Classroom although if for carrying out activities like creating assignments and grading them, it is better to use the website.

2. Once you are signed in, you can then proceed to select between being a student and a teacher. Go on to select 'I'm a Teacher'.

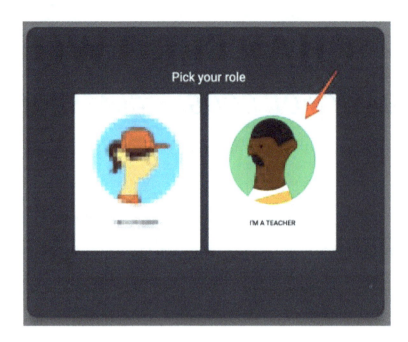

3. The next step is to create your class. At the top right corner of the Google Classroom home page is a '+' sign for creating your class. Select the '+' sign and then proceed to click on 'Create class'.

This dialog box helps you to select between creating your own class and joining an already existing class. Google Classroom asks schools or institutions to make use of the G Suite for Education. This is to make sure the teachers and students are provided with more secure measures and enough privacy if the Google Classroom is to be used in actual classrooms. For those using the Google Classroom for personal or home use however, you do not have to be bothered about this.

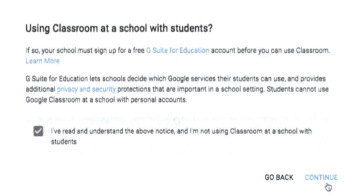

4. The next process after this is to create your class. This new box is where you will fill in details like your class name, the section (in case you want to create different classes for different sections), the subject to be taught and your class room number (the location). Note that only the class name is required, other options are optional and you do not have to fill them.

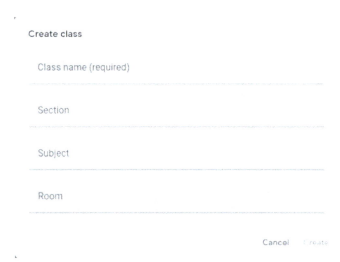

5. You should then proceed to select 'Create'. You should then click on 'Got it' and then your Google Classroom is created and ready for you.

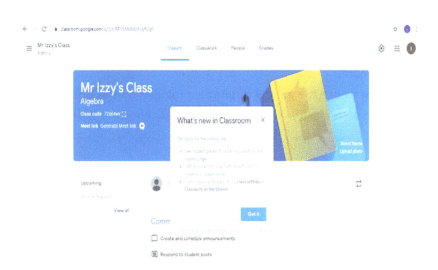

On the Google Classroom home page, there are three main tabs identified which are Stream, Classwork, People and Grades.

Stream: Stream allows you to plan your class tasks (assignments) and if you want to make class announcements. You may decide to include new assignments having materials attached to them and also dates for which they will be due. The left is to notify you of upcoming assignments. A message can also be delivered to the whole class by using social media services. The message may or may not include attachments.

Classwork: The classwork tab is where you assign your works, create assignments and questions, have your works organized into units or modules using topics and organize your work the way you want it to appear to your students.

People: This tab is dedicated to helping you manage your students. From here, your students can be invited to your classroom and also have their level of permissions managed. In the process of inviting students to your class, they must be set up in your Google Apps for Education as Google contacts. If they are not set up, you can then use the school directory.

Grades: This tab is for showing the grades of your students when assignments have been turned in. This also shows the schedule of your students at the end of the term.

Customizing your Google Classroom

Google Classroom assigns a default header image and theme once you are creating your class for the first time. Once students click your classroom for announcements or assignments sake, this header is what your students will be seeing. You can however decide to customize this header and have it changed to suit your choice.

1. Drag your mouse over the banner image.
2. The 'Select Theme' option is found in the bottom right corner of the banner image. You should then click on it.
3. Selecting this opens you up to a new gallery of photos. You can then select any of them that appeal to you. There are however a wide range of varieties that you can choose from although they have been grouped on some kind of academic subjects. You can select from General, English & History, Math & Science, Arts and more.

    You can decide not to use the gallery of photos provided by the Google Classroom but instead import photos from your own gallery. Click on the 'Upload Photo' option which is just below the 'Select Theme' option.

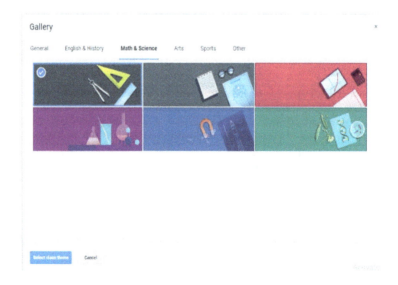

4. Once you have decided on which photo to choose, you should then click on it and then select the 'Select Class Theme' option.

Asides from having the theme of your Google Classroom changed, you can also proceed to change the photo on the profile of your classroom. The following steps give you a breakdown of how to do this:

1. Select the 'Menu' option located at the top left corner of the Google Classroom home page.
2. Scroll down to reveal the 'Settings' option. Select the option 'Settings'
3. There is the 'Change' option under the 'Profile Picture' tab. Select this 'Change' option.

4. You can then proceed to select the 'Select a photo from your computer' option. You can also go about this by having a photo dragged from the gallery of your computer.

5. The box can then be resized over your photo. This can however be done if you wish to as it is optional.
6. You can then select the 'Set as profile photo' option.

Once you are satisfied with the theme and profile of your classroom, you can then proceed to manage and create a syllabus for your Google Classroom.

Adding a Syllabus

To add syllabus to your class, you should select the tab labelled Classwork. The steps to adding what you want in your classroom are highlighted below:

1. Once you are on the class that you want, select the Classwork tab.
2. Click on the 'Create' option and then select the 'Material' option.

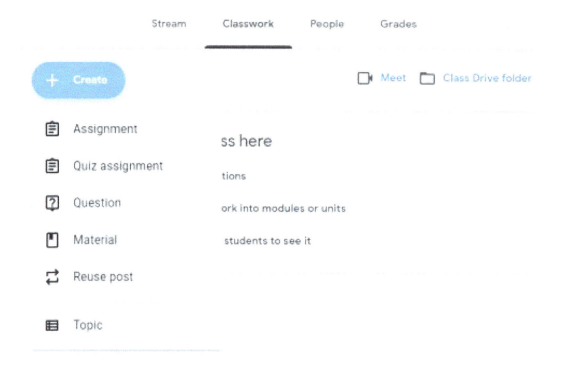

Selecting this makes a dialog box pop up with options which indicate that you can choose when you want your post to be shared with your class.

3. You should then proceed to add a title and description (which is optional). You can also add attachments if you think they are necessary.
4. Click on the 'Topic' option and have your materials assigned to a new topic and name it 'Syllabus'.
5. Once you are done with this, you should then click on 'Post'

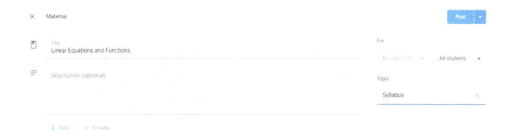

It is possible to have your materials assigned to more than one class if it is required or even assigned to individuals. The option is available when creating new Material for your class at the top left corner.

To get your Syllabus Topic at the top of your Classwork page, you should click on the 3 arrows located at the top right corner of the 'Topic' option and then click on the 'Move Up' option. You can repeat this until you are satisfied at the position. Another means of achieving this is to select and hold your Topics or Materials and dragging them up and down on the Classwork page until you find a suitable position.

Class Resource Page

This helps you to be able to access the resources available in a particular class in your Google Classroom. The steps include:

1. Select the particular class that you want to assess.
2. Select the 'About' option located at the top

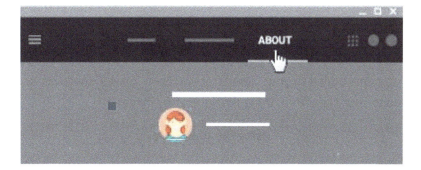

3. This opens you to an array of options from which you can click on any. The options include: Your work, Class Drive folder, Classroom calendar, Google Calendar. The functions of the options are highlighted below:

   - Your work - This option gives you access to work that has been done by you in the glass when you click on it.

- Class Drive folder – Clicking on this option allows you to be able to have access to the contents of the class.
- Classroom calendar –This option allows you to be able to access the calendar of your assignments when you click on it.
- Google Calendar- Once you select this option, you can the access the calendar of assignments on your Google Calendar.

Notifications

It is possible for you to either have your notifications turned on or not. The steps involved include:

1. Select the 'Menu' option located at the top left corner of the Google Classroom home page.
2. Scroll down to reveal the 'Settings' option. Select the option 'Settings'
3. You can then turn on or off any notifications that you have clicked on.

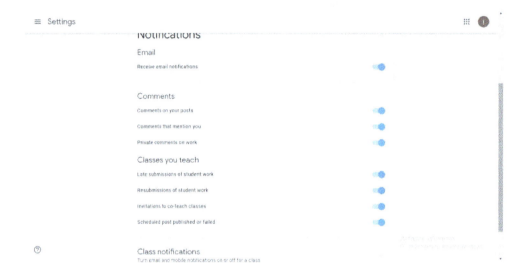

4. The 'Receive email notifications' option served the purpose of having all of the notifications turned off once you select the 'Turn off' icon located at the front of the option.

Adding Students to your Google Classroom

It is important to have students added to your class after you have created the classroom. There are two ways of having students added to your classroom; using the code or by invitation.

Using the class code

The first step is to have the students register by themselves by using the class code. The class code is a short code that is generated by the Google Classroom and this will allow anyone who is aware of it to join the class. To access the code, you have to go through this:

1. Click on the 'Class Settings' options located at the top right corner.

2. Scroll down to the 'General' sub- section and you will find the code. You can then copy or write it down and share to your students.

3. Your students should then go to the website *classroom.google.com,* select the '+' icon located at the top right corner of the Google Classroom home page. They should then proceed to select the 'Join class' option.

4. Your students should then input the class code that must have been provided to them and they will get automatically added to your classroom.

The teacher can reset the code at any given time or even decide to have the code disabled. You can do this by going to the settings option where you got the code and click on the drop- down button beside the code. This then offers options such as Display, Copy, Reset and Disable.

By Invitation

This way involves the teacher adding the students manually. This is not as stressful as you might envisage and is rather straight and easy. This method involves the following steps:

1. Select the tab 'People' found at the top of the Google Classroom page.

2. Select the 'Invite Students' option (the + sign found in front of students).
3. This makes a dialog box pop up which provides where you should input the email addresses of your students or Google Groups. You should then select the 'Invite' option found at the bottom.

4. This will then send a link to your student's email which invites them directly to the Google Classroom.

It is necessary to be aware that when the teacher is making use of the G Suite for Education, only students who are a part of the teachers Google domain can be added. Students making use of Gmail accounts that are public will not have access to the Google Classroom online content as this is intentionally done. This is part of the security and privacy move offered by Google to help the students and teachers using the Google Classroom platform.

Co- teachers in your Google Classroom

Adding a co-teacher to your Google Classroom

It is sometimes necessary for you to have a co- teacher in your class hence the Google Classroom offers the feature of inviting one. It is also possible to add a group of co- teachers to your Google Classroom although this can only be achievable if you make use of Google Groups. Using the G Suite would limit the possibility of adding co- teachers from other schools to your classroom but allows you to add co- teachers from your own school.

Why add co- teachers?

Co- teachers have the ability to perform almost as much as all tasks as the main teacher including:

- Creation of assignments
- Writing feedbacks on works submitted by the students
- Grade the works of the students
- Make announcements or posts for the whole class to see using the 'Stream'
- Access the Google Drive folder of the class
- Send both students and teachers email

However, there is a limit to what the co- teacher can do when compared to the main teacher including:

- Deleting a class
- Having the main teacher removed from the class
- Having another teacher in the class on mute

Inviting a co- teacher

If you are in a Google Group, you do not have to be the owner of such Google Group. In fact, you do not have to be a member. All you need is to have access to see the group members and also their email addresses.

1. Visit *classroom.google.com*
2. Select which of the classes it is that the co- teacher or the group is to join
3. Select the 'People' option located at the top.
4. Select the 'Invite teachers' option. You can proceed to invite a group or just an individual.

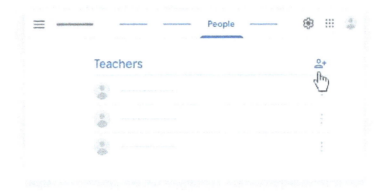

5. The email address of the teacher or the group should then be entered. Google Classrooms help to suggest addresses that match the one you are typing in so as to ease you.
6. Select a teacher or a group from the list shown.
7. You can repeat steps 5 & 6 if you have more teachers to be invited.
8. Select the 'Invite' option.

Removing a co- teacher

Co- teachers can be removed by both the main teacher and other co- teachers. However if the Google Drive folder of the class is owned by the co- teacher to be removed, it is important for another teacher to be made the owner of the folder before the c0- teacher is then removed. For a main teacher to leave a class, the main teacher has to leave as a co- teacher after making another co- teacher the new owner of the class. No main teacher can be removed from a class.

1. Visit *classroom.google.com*
2. Select which of the classes it is that the co- teacher or the group is to join
3. Select the 'People' option located at the top
4. Select the 'Move' option located in front of the name of the co- teacher.

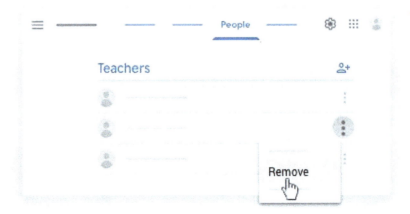

5. To confirm this, select the 'Remove' option.

Getting invited as a co- teacher

Whenever you have been invited by another teacher to come and co- teach a class, you will get notified in your email. The email comes with a link which automatically helps you to accept once you click on the link. You can also join by logging in to the Google Classroom and selecting the 'Accept' option found on the card of the inviting class.

Transferring class ownership

Only the main teacher can transfer the ownership of a class to a co- teacher and then this makes the co- teacher the main teacher. There can only be one main teacher in a class hence when the co- teacher accepts the transfer of ownership, they automatically become the new own and main teacher while you become a co- teacher. You will no longer have the power to delete the class and other powers associated with the main teacher as only the new main teacher can do that.

Who can receive ownership transfer?

- As the main teacher who is making use of a G Suite account or a G Suite for Education account, only a co- teacher using that same account type can receive the transfer of ownership hence another co- teacher using a personal Google account cannot receive the transfer of ownership.
- As a main teacher that uses a personal Google account, it is only balanced that only a co- teacher with a Personal Google account can receive ownership transfer and you cannot transfer ownership to a teacher using G Suite account or G Suite for Education account.

Who owns the class material after transfer?

Once the class ownership has been transferred, the new main teacher owns:

- The class Google Drive folder
- Class templates folder and the materials in it
- Student works that have been turned in

Who owns the deleted class materials after transfer?

Deleted files remain the property of the previous main teacher only if they run the Google Classroom with a G Suite for Education account and if the files had been deleted before they transferred ownership.

How to transfer class ownership

1. Visit *classroom.google.com*
2. Select which of the classes it is that is to be transferred to another teacher
3. Select the 'People' option located at the top
4. Select the 'More' > 'Make class owner' option which is located in front of the name of the teacher.
5. Select the 'Invite' option.

A message confirming when the transfer has been done will be sent to your email.

In a situation where you do not want to go ahead with the transfer of ownership anymore and the teacher has not confirmed the invitation, you can decide to have the invitation cancelled and retracted. The following steps should be taken:

1. Visit *classroom.google.com*
2. The class in which the transfer of ownership is about to take place should then be selected
3. Select the 'People' option located at the top
4. Select the 'More' > 'Remove invite to own' option which is located in front of the name of the teacher.

Accepting or declining transfer ownership invitation

If you have been invited by a teacher to take over the ownership of a class, you will receive a notification in your email. You can then proceed to respond by either accepting or declining y the following steps:

1. Select the 'Respond' option that comes with the invitation email
2. Select the 'Accept' or 'Decline' option.

Once you have agreed to take over the ownership of a class, emails are sent to both of the parties (you and the initial owner of the class) to confirm that the transfer has been done.

Class size for teachers and students

This depends on the account type that your Classroom operates on. There are two kinds of accounts that the Google Classroom allows; G Suite for Education and the Personal Google Accounts.

G Suite for Education

- This does not allow for more than twenty (20) teachers at a time. You can however send invitation to more than 20 teachers but only 20 is allowed to join.
- This also allows for not more than 1000 members in total (including both students and teachers).
- This also allows you to be a member of up to a thousand (1000) classes. There is also no limit to the amount of classes that you can create.
- Once you have created your class, you can begin to send out invitations in bulk to both students and teachers. You can send up to 500 invitations per day to students for every teacher.
- You can also add 20 guardians per student with this account. All the email addresses are also visible to the teacher.

Personal Google Accounts

- This does not allow for more than twenty (20) teachers at a time. You can however send invitation to more than 20 teachers but only 20 is allowed to join.
- This however does not allow for more than 250 members (including both students and teachers).
- When using a personal Google Account, teachers are also limited in the activities that they can partake in, including creation of classes and invitation of students.
- This account only lets you join 100 classes while using the Google Classroom. You can only join 30 per day. You are also limited in the amount of classes you can create, although you can only create 30 per day.
- Upon creating your class, you can only send 100 invitations per day for every teacher in the class.
- This feature however does not support inviting guardians in other to share email summaries with them. The email addresses are also not visible with this account type.

Copy, Edit, Archive

On creating a class, you might realize you have made some mistakes or you want to make some changes to your classroom, this sub-section show you how to go about it. The following steps are involved:

1. Select the menu button located at the top left corner of your Google Classroom home page.
2. Proceed to click on the 'Classes' option. This shows you all the classes that have been created by you.

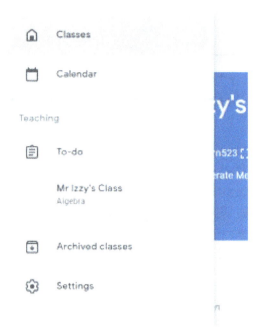

3. The classes you have created will then appear. Proceed and click the 3 dots that are at the top right corner of the class you choose to edit.
4. Select either of the 3 options 'Edit', 'Copy' or 'Archive'.

The Edit button is for having your class renamed. It also helps to change your section, subject or the classroom number. The Copy button is to have your classes organized and reordered in the dashboard. The Archive button allows you to archive your class by removing it from the dashboard. Once archived, the class no longer appears in the dashboard but can only be accessed by selecting the menu option and clicking on the 'Archived Classes' option. Once accessed from here, you can choose to restore the archived class or have it permanently deleted.

Communication in the Classroom

Communicating in the classroom can take two forms majorly the **Stream** and the **Email. The Stream** is like a Facebook message wall in which all the members of the class can see the message. Both the teachers and students can access this feature. This also comes handy as they serve as a kind of reminder, notifies students of events that are upcoming or other materials or events that the teacher wants the whole class to be aware of. This can be put to use by navigating to the tab 'Stream' and then click on the dialog box 'Share something with your class…'.

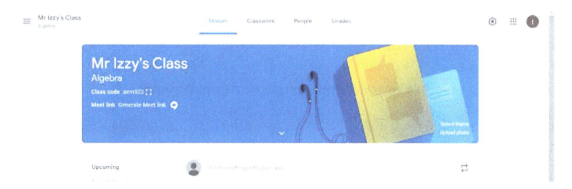

Once you are done with typing in whatever you want to share with the class, you can also decide to add attachments and then you can select the 'Post' option.

The second way is by using **Email.** There is a 3- dot option that appears next to the teachers name on the class homepage which the students should click on in other to access a Gmail message which is directed automatically to the teachers email address. In other to message other students, a student can select the tab 'People' and as usual, there is a 3- dot in front of every student's name. The student should then click on that and select 'Email Student'.

This is also available to teachers once they select the 'People' tab and even have the added option of making multiple selection of students and selecting the **Actions>Email** if they want the message to be seen by a group of students.

Asides from communication between teacher and students and then students and students, you can also communicate with the parents or guardians of your students. The Google Classroom provides an added feature that lets the guardians and parents of your students to get notified of summaries of their children's activities by email. Upcoming works, missing works and activities in the class are among the summaries that parents and guardians get notified of. Google Classroom helps to automatically generate these summaries as they cannot be personalized with messages from the teacher or include extra contents. For parents who are interested in getting notified of these summaries, they can decide on what basis they want to receive emails be it on a daily basis or weekly basis. Parents who are not interested can also unsubscribe from the notifications.

Only students using the G Suite for Education school accounts can have class summaries and it is also important for the teachers to be granted access by the administrators at the school to these email summaries and also be able to manage them.

Making Comments on Announcements

When teachers post announcements, it is normal to get back comments from students. Teachers also can make comments on posts or even make comments on other student's comments. The following steps are taken:

1. Navigate to the 'Stream' tab on the homepage of your Google Classroom.
2. Once the teacher has made a post on the 'Stream' tab, there is a 'Add class comment' box under the post in which you can input your comment to be posted on the stream.

3. Once you are done with typing your comment, you can then select the 'post' option and this helps to send your comment to the 'Stream' tab and under the post and this is made available to the whole class.

Student Permissions

For orderliness in a classroom, it is necessary to control how students can share posts and make comments. This is even a thing in physical classes as students have to take permissions before they can make contributions in the class otherwise the whole class will be rowdy and disorderly. Setting permission helps the teacher to manage how much students in the Classroom can share posts and make comments. Permissions can either be set by student or by class. Students can delete their posts once you make posting and commenting possible however they cannot have their comments or posts edited. Any post or comment can however be deleted by the teacher.

Postings by students in the Classroom

- Post – This goes on the class stream as questions or information. An example is 'When is the next excursion to the zoo?
- Comment – This is a response to a post or a comment. An example of this is 'The excursion is indefinite because the zoo has not been opened in a while'.
- Reply – This is a response to a comment in which the person who made the comment has their name mentioned. An example is '+ Commenter's name Thanks for the information'.

Setting up Email Summaries

Only teachers or administrators can access this. Guardians can be invited by either the administrator or the teacher to have automatic email summaries showing the progress of their children delivered to their email. The classes to be included in the summary are chosen by you (the teacher). Only students who are registered with a G Suite account can have their guardians added.

To have access to inviting guardians, removing them or sending emails to them:

- The Google Classroom admin would have to verify if you are a teacher or not, turn on the summaries and then the permission to manage the summaries will be handed to you
- You should make use of the web Classroom version or the Android version to invite the guardians

Turning the guardian summaries on or off

1. Visit *classroom.google.com*
2. Select the option 'class' > Settings
3. The General tab has the switch 'On' or 'Off' options
4. There is the 'Add all the classes you teach to guardian email summaries' option and you can select this if you want to have the summaries for all of your classes turned on (this is however optional).

Select the 'Add Class' option.

Inviting a guardian

The guardian should only be invited by just a teacher or one of the school administrators. The guardian automatically gets linked to all of the classes that the student is a member of, once they accept the invitation from the teacher. The guardian of the student is however visibly seen by teachers and admin that are verified.

1. Visit *classroom.google.com*
2. Select the option 'class' > People
3. Select the 'Invite guardians' option found in front of the name of the student
4. The email address of the guardian should then be entered. Commas should be placed after each email address when multiple guardians are been invited.
5. Select the 'Invite' option.

Removing a guardian

It should be noted that once the guardian is invited, he becomes added to all of the classes that the child is registered to, hence once the guardian is removed, the action makes sure that the guardian is not only removed from a particular class, but all of the class that the student might be in. Guardians who are no longer interested in getting emails should unsubscribe from their end rather than risk being removed from the whole school.

1. Visit *classroom.google.com*
2. Select the option 'class' > People
3. Select the 'More' option and > Remove guardians option found in front of the name of the student
4. Select the 'Remove' option found in the boxes located in front of the guardian's name.

The guardian who has been removed, the student and also the teacher who removed the guardian all get an email of confirmation once the guardian has been removed.

Sending Email to guardians

The teacher can send emails directly to the guardian if they accept the invitation to have email summaries automatically sent to them.

1. Visit *classroom.google.com*
2. Select the option 'class' > People
3. There are a couple of options for you to choose from:
   - Select the 'More' > Email guardians' option found in front of the name of the student; this is to send an email to the guardian of one parent. There is an email window that pops up having in the field 'To' the address of the email.
   - Click on the 'Email All Guardians' located at the top if the email is to be sent to the guardians of all the students in your class.
4. Your subject and message should then be entered
5. Select the 'Send' option.

CHAPTER 3

ASSIGNMENTS AND GOOGLE FORMS

Creating an Assignment in your Google Classroom

The Google Classroom serves the purpose of creating assignments and having them assigned to students.

1. Select the tab 'Classwork'. This tab allows you to access on- going assignments and already submitted ones and you can also create new assignments.
2. Click on the 'Create' option and then select the 'Assignment' option.

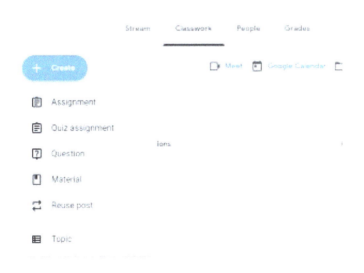

There are also other options like Question, Material which are used if you want to ask your students a single question or if you want to simply post an attachment or visuals.

3. You should then title your assignment in the box provided and include descriptions or instructions which are optional.
4. There is a lot of flexibility offered here by the Google Classroom platform while creating your assignments as you have options like due date (you might also include due time if you want) and how many points the assignment will be marked over.

5. Once you are done with this, you should then select the 'Assign' option fond at the top right corner.

Your students will receive messages in their email notifying them of new assignments once you click on the 'Assign' option. If you decide to share the assignment to not just one class but more, you should then select at the top left corner of the assignment window the name of the class you want and then click on all of the classes that you want to share the assignment with.

All of your assignments are taken by the Google Classroom and are added automatically to your Google Calendar. While still on the ''Classwork' tab, you can select the Google Calendar in order to have a proper view of your schedule and due dates of your assignments.

Assignments and Google Documents

It is not uncommon for teachers to want to have attachments added to their assignments. This can however be done by added attachments saved to your Drive. These attachments always come in handy especially when they are study guides, instructions which are lengthy or other materials. To add such attachments; click on the symbol 'Add' below the box for instructions (the symbol is right before the 'Create' option).

On selecting the 'Add' symbol, various types of attachments pop out and you get to select the one you want. The attachment options include 'Google Drive', 'Link', 'File' and 'YouTube'.

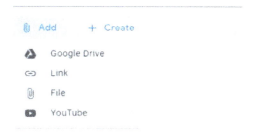

- Selecting the 'Google Drive' option helps you access files that have been stored in your Google Drive. Once you have found the file, you should then click on it.
- Selecting the 'Link' option allows you to be able to have the link pasted in the Link box made available.
- Selecting the 'File' option having the paper clip icon gives you access to files that have been stored on your computer storage. Once you have found your file, double click on it so as to select it.
- Selecting the 'YouTube' option directs you to 'YouTube' where you can then search for the video you want to post using the search bar. Once you have found the video, you should click on it.

Once you are done with selecting the attachment, you can then proceed to select how you want your students to interact with it.

Click on the drop down button which then reveals 3 further options.

Each of these 3 types of interactions has their various importance's which are highlighted below:

- **Students can view file:** This option should be the suitable one for you if your purpose is to make all your students to have access to this file without being able to make changes or modification to it. This is great when you are attaching study guides and generic handouts which are to be made available to the whole class.

- **Students can edit file:** This choice is most useful when you have a document that your students are required to fill out or work on as a group or together. If all your students are allowed to work on the same documents, this is the option for you as they will be able to edit with this option. This is definitely perfect for a collaborative group project in which students are busy with a particular Google Presentation but different slides or when you need them to discuss a topic for the next class and they have to brainstorm in advance.

- **Make a copy for each student:** In this option, each document will be duplicated and there will be a copy of the original that has been created by this option, hence the student can individually complete the copied document. The original copy is still kept intact as the students do not have access to it. In a situation where you have a document that you quickly need to pass on to the students so that they can start working on it or where they have to fill their answers in the provided blanks, this option is ideal for your use.

Assignments using Topics

The Google Classroom also has the feature of using the topic to organize assignments. This is effective when both teachers and students are trying to locate various assignments as this helps to have the assignments grouped by type or unit under the tab 'Classwork'. Topics are also useful as they help to have your contents into organized units.

1. Select the Classwork tab and then click on the 'Create' option.
2. Select the 'Topic' option from the open tab.

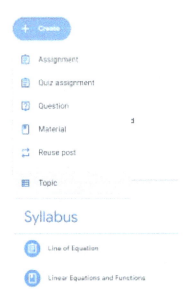

3. Add a name for your topic and select the 'Add' option.

You can also have your new assignments added to a Topic. Select the drop- down button beside the Topic just before assigning it. If you want to move already created assignments to a Topic, the following steps are necessary:

1. Select the Classwork tab
2. On the assignment to be moved, click on the 3 dots
3. Select the Edit option
4. Click on the drop- down option beside the Topic and then select the Topic you want the assignment to move to.

Google Forms in Google Classrooms

Surveys, forms for feedback, sign- ups and a lot more are part of the inevitable of teaching hence the need to understand Google Forms and its uses. Google Classroom also makes use of quizzes which are created by the Google Forms. The Google Formal so includes a wide range of different types of question for quizzes and also you can customize the settings.

Quizzes: You have to first create a basic form before you can proceed to create your own quiz. To create your blank basic form, find your way to the Google Forms homepage or visit the website *docs.google.com/forms/,* then select the 'Blank' icon.

It is essential to change some of the settings on your form before proceeding to writing your questions. Select the 'Settings' icon located at the top right corner of your Google Forms homepage.

Select the tab for Quiz and make sure the 'Make this a quiz' option is toggled on. This provides various forms of quiz from which you can choose from.

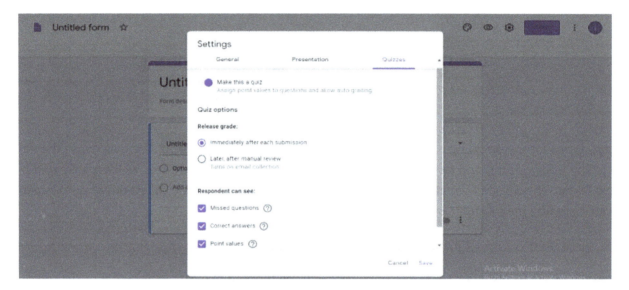

Customize these options at your discretion and select the 'Save' option at the bottom right corner. Your quiz should then be named after which you can proceed to set out your questions.

There should however be a correct answer for each question on your quiz. Select the 'Answer Key' option in other to set the correct answer.

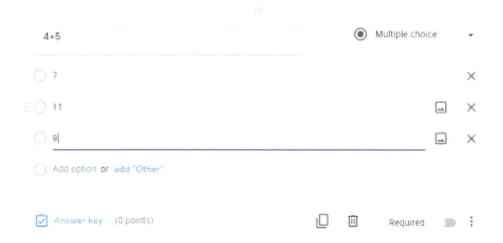

- For multiple choice questions, you should then proceed to select the correct answer from the multiple choices available.

- For short- answer questions, there is an 'Add a correct answer' box for the correct answer and you can go ahead and include other multiple answers that are correct in case a word is different. Ticking 'Mark all other answers incorrect' will automatically mark the answers that do not tally incorrect. If left not ticked, answers that look not exactly similar will be left for you to review manually and have them graded.

- For paragraph questions, there is no opportunity to provide the question with correct answers. The teacher has to grade them by reading the answers one by one because they are always lengthy and full of extra analysis.

Once the correct answers have been input and identified, it is necessary to click on the 'how many points' option so as to attach a worth to the questions.

There is also the opportunity of giving feedback to assignments by selecting the 'answer feedback'.

○ 9   ✓

📋 Add answer feedback

Done

This allows students to receive feedback on questions although these feedbacks are dependent on if they answer the questions correctly or not. Select the 'Add answer feedback' option and input the feedback that would be made visible for both answers that are correct or incorrect.

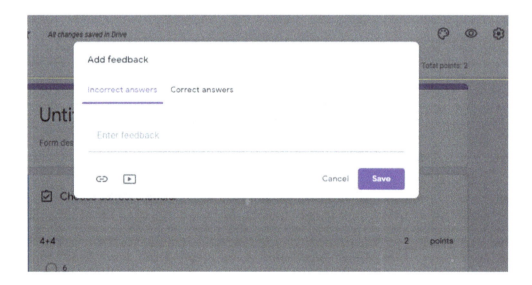

After setting all of your questions, you can proceed to preview it in other to confirm your satisfaction. Select the 'Preview' option at the top right corner. The Preview option is represented by the eye symbol.

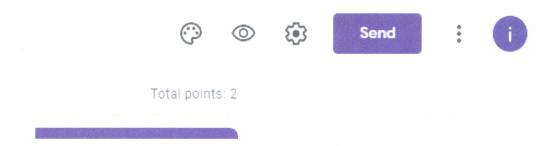

Total points: 2

Sections of your quiz

This can be done by having your quiz separated into two or more sections although this is determined by the amount of questions you have available. This also helps to break your questions across a couple of pages rather than have all of them clustered on just a page.

Having your quiz sectioned can be done by selecting the 'Add section' option available in the toolbar located on the side and is represented by two small horizontal bars.

The instructions above can also be used to have questions added to the sections. Moving questions from one section to another is done by holding the cursor over such questions and having it dragged to the proposed section.

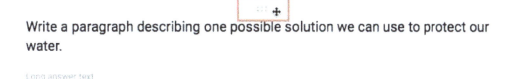

Write a paragraph describing one possible solution we can use to protect our water.

Long answer text

Upon creating your quiz, it is then important to have it transferred to your Google Classroom to your students. Forms can be attached to your assignments the same way in which links, videos and documents are attached to it.

Once you have clicked on the 'Add' option while creating your assignment, select the 'Google Drive' option.

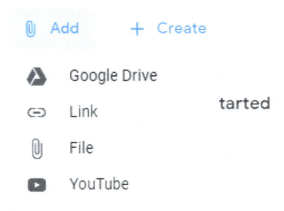

Upon finding your quiz, select the quiz and then click on Add.

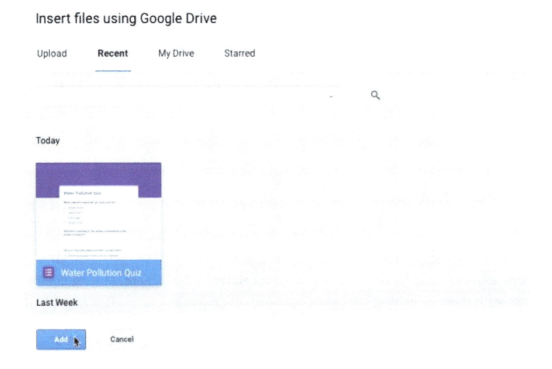

Once the assignment which has the quiz attached has been sent, it will then be available for your students to complete. Responses can be accessed just like you are using Google Forms.

Completion and Submission of Assignments by Students

Active assignments are available to students once they are logged on to the Google Classrooms. All they have to do is click on a class that they belong to and then have the upcoming assignments reviewed. A better way to however do this is to select the 'Menu' option located at the top left corner and select the 'To- do' option.

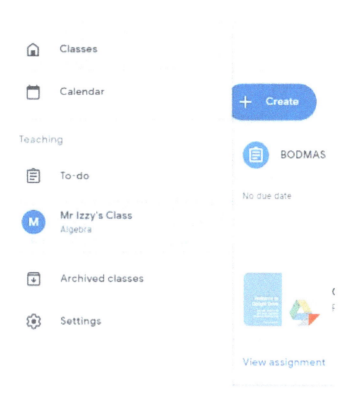

On selecting the 'To- do' option from the pop- down menu, this makes visible to the student as list of assignments for each of the classes, including the ones that have been submitted, those that are yet to be submitted and those that are past their due dates. Once the teacher has graded an assignment, it will be visible in this tab to along with the grade obtained appearing with them.

The student's relevant file will be visible once any of the assignments is clicked on. An extra button close to the Share button is included to the toolbar located at the top right corner if the relevant file is a Google Drive file. This is the 'Turn it in' button. The assignment is submitted to the teacher once the student clicks on it.

There is no confirmed way to have the YouTube videos or URLs which teachers have assigned to their students turned in for now, although there are steps to change that already.

Grading, Returning and Feedback on Assignments

Assignments are available to the teachers for grading and review once they have been submitted by the students. Each assignment is given a page of its own by Google Classroom and this no doubt eases the grading, review and leaving of feedbacks for the students. Assignments submitted to the teachers by the students can be found in different ways. Entering a class of interest and selecting the name of the assignment for grading from the Stream view is one of the most effective and efficient ways of finding student submissions. Once it is observed that conversations between students get the assignments lost and not easily found, the sidebar located at the top left of the Stream view contains the 'Upcoming Assignments' box which helps you located the buried assignments. The assignments you want to grade should be selected and the following steps followed:

1. Select the 'Classwork' tab and then click on the assignment that is to be graded and then select the 'View Assignment' option.

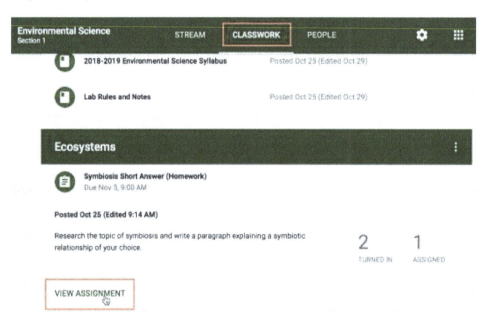

2. This makes visible the Student Work page for your assignment. You can then proceed to access the submissions of each student and then have them graded.

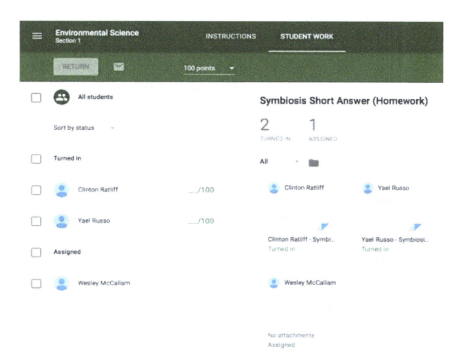

3. On selecting a student's submission, you can make use of the Drives commenting feature to make enough feedbacks on certain aspects of the submitted work of the student There is automatic save for whatever changes are made hence the document can be closed immediately.
4. On the Classroom page at the students right hand side is a box saying 'No grade'. This is where the graded points from the assignment should be entered.
5. The box next to the just graded student should be ticked and the blue 'Return' button should be clicked in order to have the grade saved and this is a notification to the student that grading of their paper has occurred.
6. Extra feedbacks should be included in the pop-up box and the 'Return Assignment' option should be selected.

Assignments can not only be graded on an individual basis but also from the Student Work Page. This is done with ease as all you have to do is select the 'Score' option which is in front of the name of the student and then the teacher can 'type the grade' the student is to be given.

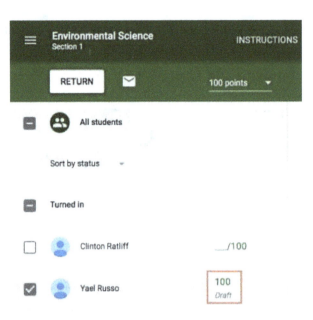

Once the assignments have been graded, it is necessary for the teacher to have them all selected and then click on the 'Return' button in order to have them delivered to the awaiting students.

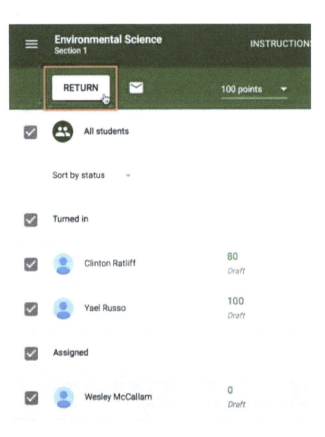

Assignments are also graded by using the grading tool.

Each submission from each student has a grading tool imbedded in them. However, you have to open the assignment first by selecting it.

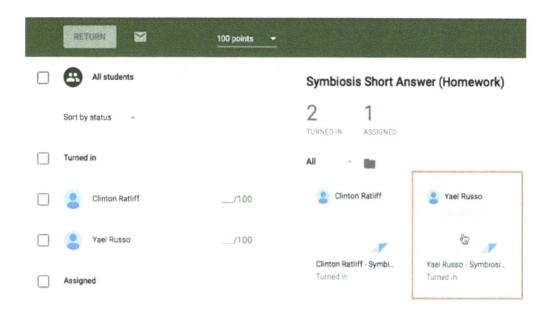

The grading tool is enclosed in a column found at the right side of the screen page. The type of grade that you wish to ascribe to a student is to be input in the 'Grade' box. Feedbacks can also be left in the field for 'Private comments' for the students to see.

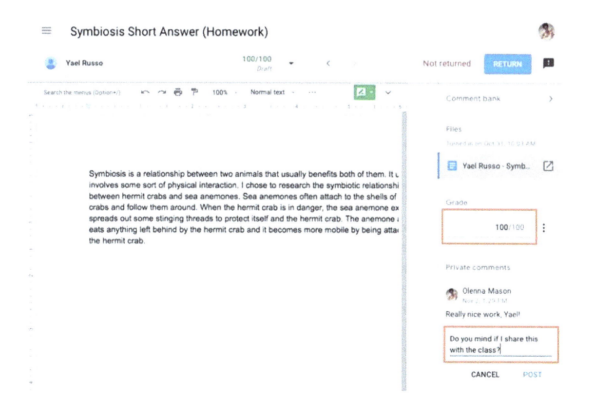

Once the assignments have been graded and it is set to be shared back to the student, the teacher should then select the assignment and click on the 'Return' option.

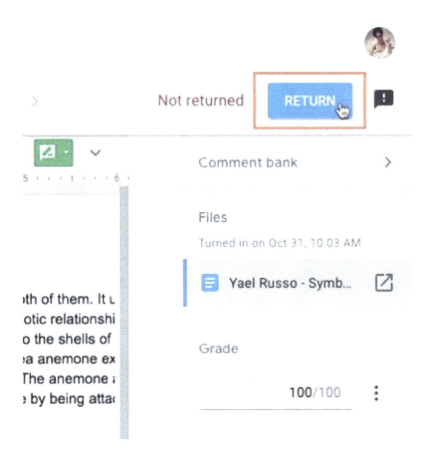

Class Grades

Grades of the whole class can be exported and moved to Google Sheets thanks to an added feature of the Google Classroom. Each assignment done by each student is created on a spread sheet which reveals all of the grades, average grades of each assignment, and the overall average grade of the whole class. Grades of assignments that have been submitted and graded by the teacher can be exported by navigating to the Student Work page and the selecting the gear icon which is located at the top right of the Student Work page and then click on the 'Copy all grades to Google Sheets' option.

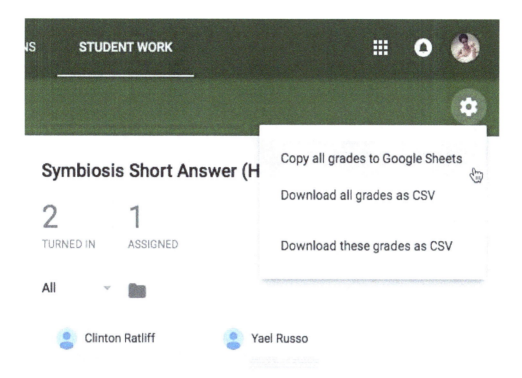

Upon having one of these spread sheets created, it is of utmost necessity to point out that this does not have any automatic update attached to it. As more assignments are graded by the teacher, it is necessary for the teacher to keep on having the newly graded assignments exported.

Tips on Grading

- Once the assignment has been graded by the teacher and returned to the student, the teacher can no longer have the documents edited for whatsoever reasons.
- Not every assignment has to be graded before the teacher can return to the student. An assignment that is not graded can be returned to a student as all the teacher has to do is make sure the box close to the name of the student is ticked and then the teacher selects the 'Return' box. Assignments submitted i error can then be returned back easily.
- There is an automatic mail notification for every student once their assignment has been returned by the teacher. This ensure that assignments are duly received and also at a timely rate. There are notifications too once new assignments have been handed out by the teachers.
- Grades can be changed at any given time by the teacher and only the teacher. This can be done by selecting the grade that is to be changed and then clicking the 'Update' option.
- All students' submitted assignments are stored in the Google Drive folder and can be easily accessed by clicking on the folder button. All of the assignments that have been submitted can then be easily reviewed at once and at a particular time.
- 100 is the default number of point for every assignment to be graded. This however is subject to change as it is flexible and depends on the teacher's grade scheme. The teacher can decide to reduce the value and click on the drop- down arrow repeatedly, or just decide to totally use a new different value, have a new value inserted or even decide that the assignment should not be scored. It all depends on the teacher.

CHAPTER FOUR

GOOGLE CLASSROOM AS A STUDENT

Signing up for the Google Classroom

A student can sign in to a Google Classroom using different types of account including the following:

- Personal Google Account – This account type can be set up for the student by the guardian or the parents. Personal accounts are however always used away from school settings such as book clubs or home schools.
- G Suite Account – This account type is set up by the administrators of organizations.
- School Account – This account type is also known as the G Suite for Education Account and is always set up by your school. The school however has to be accredited. The teacher or the IT administrator for the school will be aware of your G Suite for Education account and you should ask them if you are not aware of it.

The steps for signing in as a student are as follows:

1. Visit the site *classroom.google.com* and select the 'Go to Classroom' option.

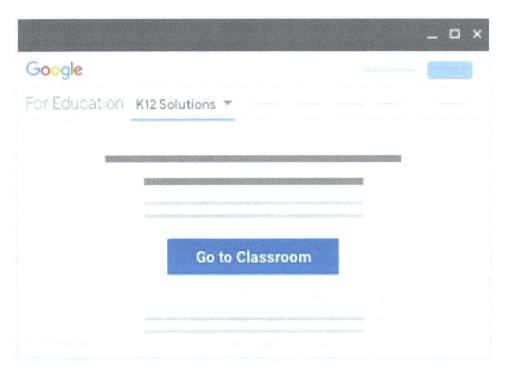

2. The email address you are willing to use to register to the Google Classroom should then be entered. Select the 'Next' option.

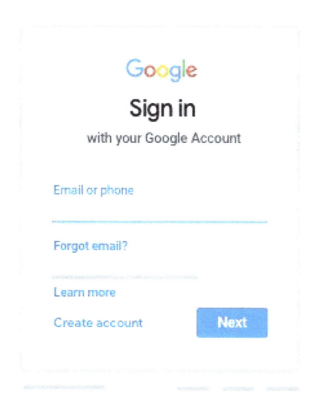

3. Your password should then be entered after which you select the 'Next' option.

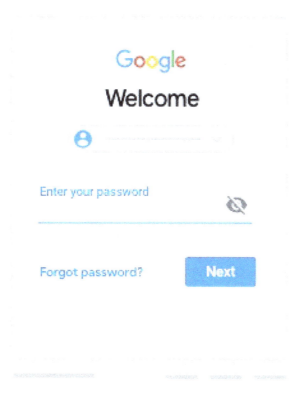

4. In case a welcome message pops up, go ahead and read the message and then proceed to select the 'Accept' option.

5. There is an icon that pops up showing two options 'I'M A STUDENT' and 'I'M A TEACHER'. Select the 'I'M A STUDENT'. This icon however shows for people using the G Suite for Education account and does not show for those using their personal Google Accounts.

6. **Select the 'Get Started' option and then you are already signed in and ready to progress to the next step.**

Joining a Class

Having access to the classroom can either be done if you have signed up on your personal computer or on your mobile device and then proceeding to joining the class. Only when you have joined your class as a student can you have access to the works posted by your teacher and then you can join conversations between the teacher and your classmates.

Joining a class can be done in two different ways:

- Using the class code – This involves you signing in to the Google classroom and then having the class code entered into the box provided for it. The class code is provided by the teacher who has created the class.
- Invitation from the teacher – Once the teacher has created the group, he or she can then send an invitation to your email. The invitation can then be accepted by clicking the link in your mail or in the Google Classroom.

If you join a particular class with your personal computer or mobile device, it does not matter if you log in with another different device, you will remain enrolled in that particular class.

Using the class code

Once the teacher has shared the class code with you, you can then proceed to join the class. You however have to follow these steps:

1. Navigate to the website *classroom.google.com*
2. Once you are signed in with your account, you can then select the '+' option located at the top right corner of the Google Classroom homepage

3. For those using the Personal Google account, selecting this '+' sign brings two options 'Join Class' and 'Create Class'. You should then select the 'Join Class' option. For those using the G Suite for Education account, selecting the '+' sign takes you directly to the dialog box in step 4.

4. A dialog box then pops up on your screen where you should then enter the class code that is provided by your classroom teacher.

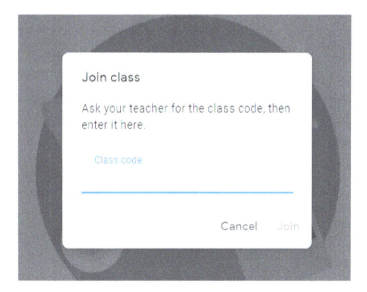

5. Click on the 'Join' option once you have entered the code.

The codes are usually combinations of both numbers and letters and not more than 6 or 7 characters and do not include spaces nor special characters.

Invitation from the teacher

Once an invitation has been sent to you by the teacher, you will get a notification of the invite in your mail and the class happens to appear on the home page of your Google classroom. The steps to follow include:

1. Navigate to the website *classroom.google.com*
2. Once you are certain that you are properly signed in with the right account, select the class card and click on the 'Join' option.

3. You are then a member of the class and can access the posts of the teachers and interact with your other students.

For any trouble joining the class, you should reach put to the teacher and inform him or her. Once you have used the code to join the class, you do not have any need of it again. In a situation where your class code does not work, you should make sure your account that you have signed in to the Google Classroom is the right one.

Completing Your Assignments

Once you have joined the class, it is necessary to understand how to go about the process of completing your assignments and submitting them for the teacher to grade. There is however different types of assignment hence this section takes you through them. The different types of assignments are PDF assignments, Video assignments and Quizzes.

Completing your PDF Assignment.

1. Select the class in which the assignment has been posted.
2. Once the assignment article has been found, select the assignment title. The assignment in this case is titled 'Sample PDF'. This assignment can be located on the Google Classroom homepage or can also be located under a topic.

Go on to click on the PDF assignment after which it redirects you to this new page where the assignment is no longer visible.

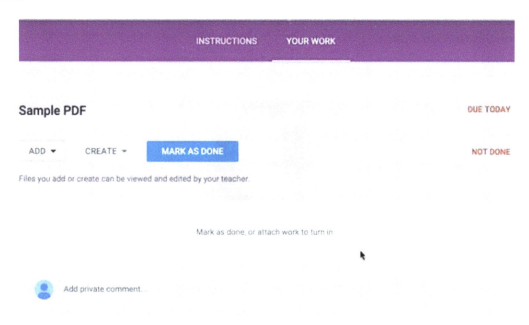

3.

4. Select the 'INSTRUCTIONS' tab located beside the 'YOUR WORK' tab so as to be able to access the assignment.

5. This then makes the PDF assignment to appear after which you can then double click on it in other to open it.

6. The PDF assignment is now open and then you should select the 'Open with' option located at the top. The option provides an array of different apps that can be used to access the assignment. They include the DocHub), the Lumin PDF, Notable PDF, Pear Deck and an option to 'Connect more apps'. We will be making use of the DocHub app.

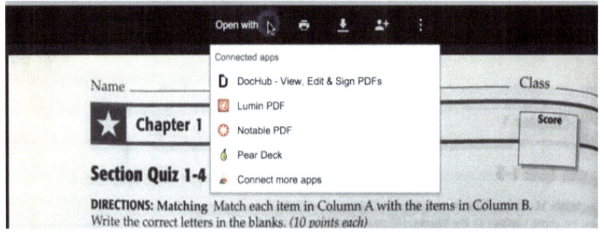

7. Click on the 'DocHub' option.

8. The PDF assignment is then opened in the DocHub app after which you should select the 'A' icon located at the top of the page towards your left side.

9.

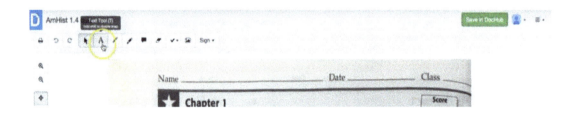

10. Clicking on the 'A' icon allows you to be able to add texts to the PDF and you can then fill in your details (Name, Date and Class) at the top of the page.

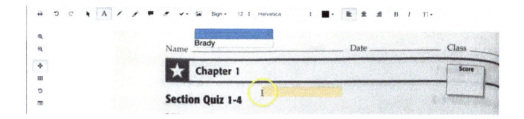

11. Yu can also select the Draw Tool located beside the 'A' icon.

12. Selecting this Draw Tool allows you to make different drawings on your assignment. For example if you want to circle options, the Draw Tool is the tool for you.

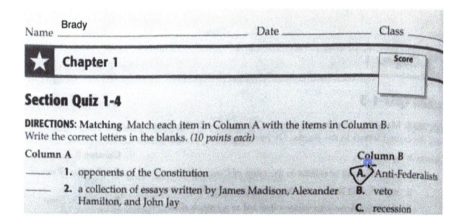

13. Once you are done with answering your PDF files and about to submit, you can then select the 'File' option located at the top right corner of your DocHub home page. The 'File' option is represented by 3 horizontal lines. You should then scroll down and select the export to 'Google Drive' option.

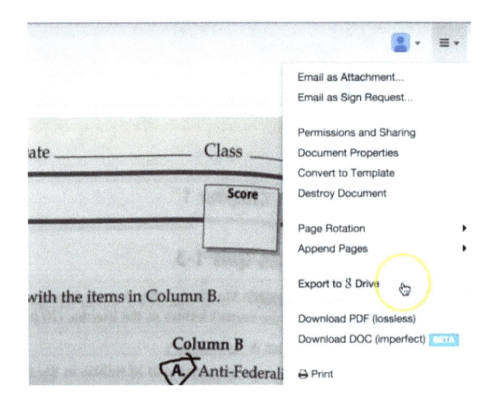

14. Your document is then successfully saved into your Google Drive, after which you can select the 'Close' option.

15. You are then redirected to your class page where you should then select 'YOUR WORK' option.

16. Selecting this then brings you to this page where you should then click on the 'Add' option in other to import the completed assignment from the Google Drive.

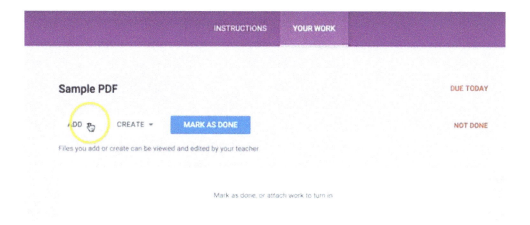

17. You can then select from the 3 options – Google Drive, Link and Upload File. Since the completed assignment was saved in the Google Drive, you should then select the 'Google Drive' option.

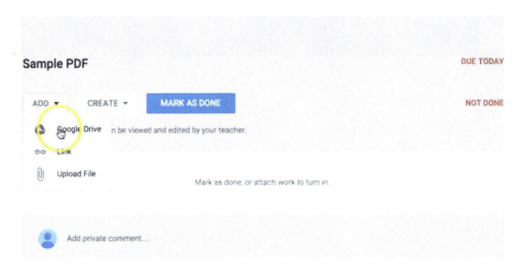

18. Selecting this directs you to the Google Drive where you can then access your completed assignments and other documents saved in your Google Drive.

19. Once you have selected the completed assignment and you have added it, you can then select the 'TURN IN' option located at the top.

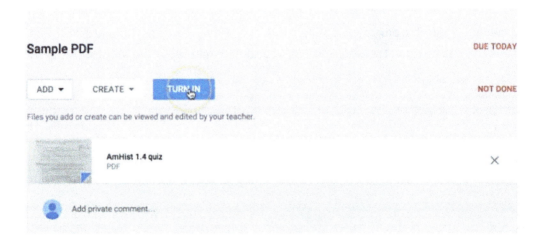

20. In a situation where you want to add additional comments to the completed assignment, you can include them in the box for 'Add private comment' before you finally click on the 'TURN IN' option again.

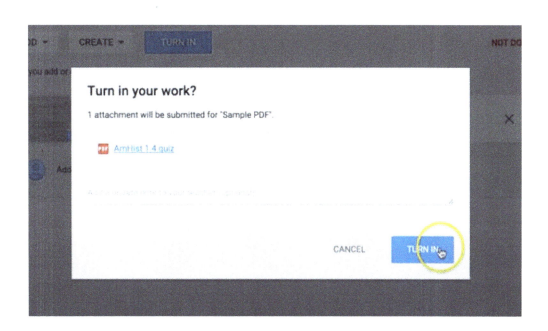

21. You are then done with the completion of your PDF assignment.

In a situation where your assignment does not require you to have any work completed nor have any file attached and all you have to do is to view the contents of the PDF assignment, you can mark your assignment as completed by clicking on the 'MARK AS DONE' option. This pops up a box where you can select the ''MARK AS DONE' option in other for your assignment to be completed.

Mark as done?

You didn't attach work for "Video", so your teacher will just see it's done.

CANCEL   MARK AS DONE

Creating a New File to Complete your Submission

1. Select the 'CREATE' option in other to have a file created from the scratch on the Google Drive. This pops up a couple of options including: Documents, Slides, Sheets and Drawings.

 Docs

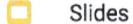 Slides

 Sheets

 Drawings

2. A file will be created for your submission once you have selected any of the options previously stated.

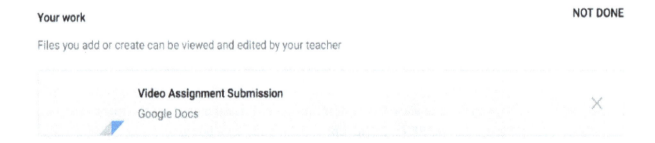

Select the file and tab that allows you to have the file edited and helps you to complete the assignment will be opened.

3. You can then proceed to click on the 'TURN IN' option located at the top right corner.

4. This then makes a box pop up asking you if you are sure about proceeding to have your work submitted. Select the 'TURN IN' option in other to have your assignment submitted.

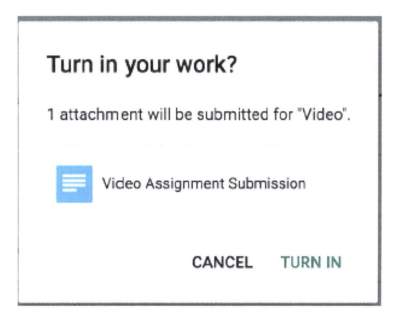

Completing your Video Assignment

1. Select the class containing the video assignment.

2. Once the assignment article has been found, select the assignment title. The assignment in this case is titled 'Video. This assignment can be located on the Google Classroom homepage or can also be located under a topic. Click on the 'OPEN' option to be able to access the video assignment.

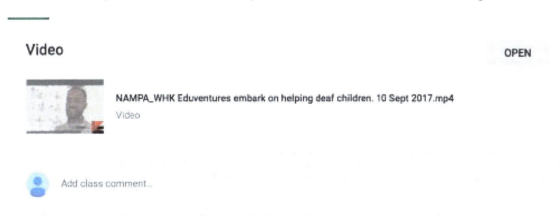

3. Selecting this then redirects you to a new page where you can include comments under the video assignment in the 'Add class comment' option. You can also send private comments in the 'Add private comment' box as this private comment will only be seen by the teacher.

Completing your assignment when there is no attached file

1. You should select the 'MARK AS Done' option if you do not have to complete your video assignment and there is no need to have any file attached.
2. This pops up another box asking you to confirm this selection. To have your video assignment marked as completed, proceed to select the 'MARK AS Done' option.

Mark as done?

You didn't attach work for "Video", so your teacher will just see it's done.

CANCEL   MARK AS DONE

Attaching a file that already exists

1. Select the 'ADD' option if you have a file that exists already and you want to have it attached to your video assignment. This 'ADD' option provides you with the following options:
   - Google Drive - Select this if your already existing file has been saved in your Google Drive and you want to import it from here.
   - Link – Select this if it is a link that you want to attach.
   - File – Select this if the already existing file has been saved on your computer or personal device and you want to import it from here.
2. Select the 'TURN IN' option once you are sure that your submission has been attached.
3. This then makes a box pop up asking you if you are sure about proceeding to have your work submitted. Select the 'TURN IN' option in other to have your assignment submitted.

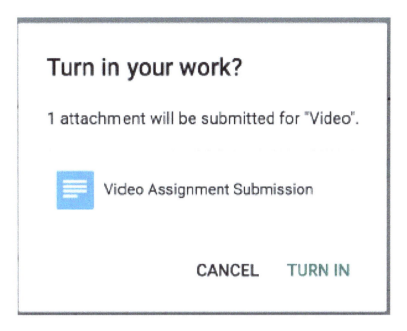

Creating a New File to Complete your Submission

1. Select the 'CREATE' option in other to have a file created from the scratch on the Google Drive. This pops up a couple of options including: Documents, Slides, Sheets and Drawings.

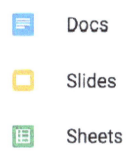

Docs

Slides

Sheets

Drawings

2. A file will be created for your submission once you have selected any of the options previously stated.

Your work

Files you add or create can be viewed and edited by your teacher

Video Assignment Submission
Google Docs

3. Select the file and tab that allows you to have the file edited and helps you to complete the assignment will be opened.

4.   You can then proceed to click on the 'TURN IN' option located at the top right corner.
5. This then makes a box pop up asking you if you are sure about proceeding to have your work submitted. Select the 'TURN IN' option in other to have your assignment submitted.

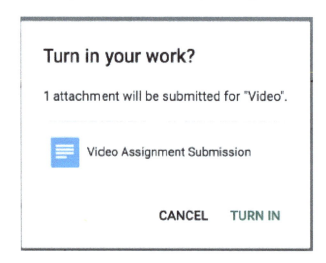

Turn in your work?

1 attachment will be submitted for "Video".

Video Assignment Submission

CANCEL   TURN IN

Completing Quizzes

This section gives you an insight of how to fill in your quiz and submit it when you are done.

1. Make sure you are properly logged in with the right account.
2. Proceed to click on the class that contains the quiz assignment in other to access it.

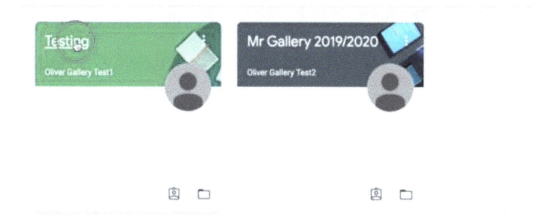

3. Once you are on the class home page, navigate to the 'Classwork' tab.

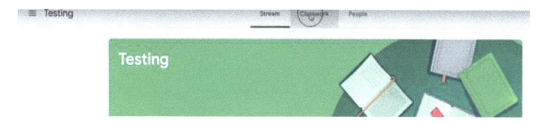

4. Once you are on the 'Classwork' tab, you can then see the quiz assignment. Click on the assignment 'Reading Assessment and Read Aloud'.

5. This then helps you properly access the quiz so you can start answering.

6. Once you select the 'Reading Assessment and Read Aloud' assignment, you can now access it and start your quiz.

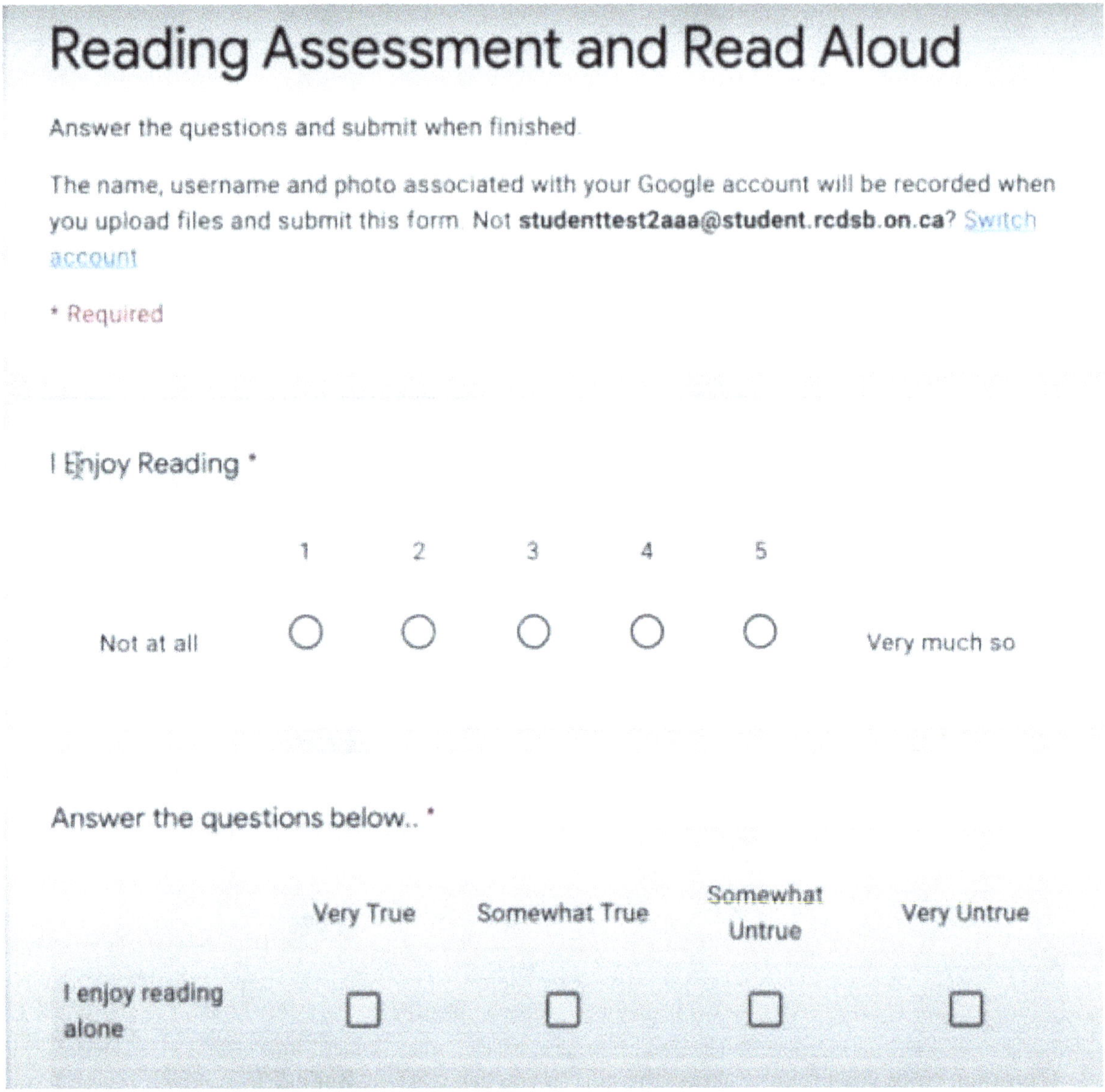

Reading Assessment and Read Aloud

Answer the questions and submit when finished.

The name, username and photo associated with your Google account will be recorded when you upload files and submit this form. Not **studenttest2aaa@student.rcdsb.on.ca**? Switch account

* Required

I Enjoy Reading *

	1	2	3	4	5	
Not at all	○	○	○	○	○	Very much so

Answer the questions below.. *

	Very True	Somewhat True	Somewhat Untrue	Very Untrue
I enjoy reading alone	☐	☐	☐	☐

7. Each question has different options and you can then select your answers by clicking on the circle or box under the option you want to choose.

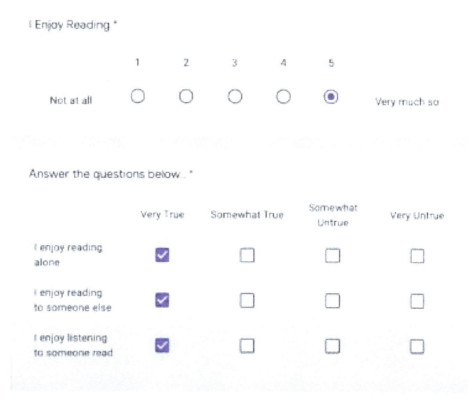

I Enjoy Reading *

	1	2	3	4	5	
Not at all	○	○	○	○	◉	Very much so

Answer the questions below.. *

	Very True	Somewhat True	Somewhat Untrue	Very Untrue
I enjoy reading alone	✔	☐	☐	☐
I enjoy reading to someone else	✔	☐	☐	☐
I enjoy listening to someone read	✔	☐	☐	☐

8. You then proceed to scroll down and answer other questions. For questions that require typing in your answers, enough space to enter in your answer is always provided hence you can input in your answer. You should then click on the 'Next' option so you can proceed to the next page.

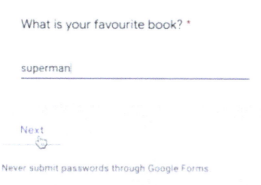

What is your favourite book? *

superman

Next

Never submit passwords through Google Forms.

9. This quiz required you to read aloud hence there is the part where you have to upload your recorded answer. Once you have recorded your audio and saved it in your Google Drive, you should then select the 'Add file' option so that you can attach the audio file.

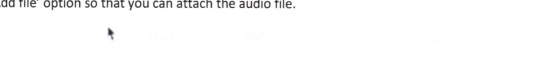

Upload a video or audio of you reading the Bad Seed *

⬆ Add file

10. Select the 'My Drive' tab located at the top of the box that pops up. You will then be able to access your audio recording along with other documents that have been saved on your drive. Select the audio recording and click on the 'Select' option so as to have the file attached.

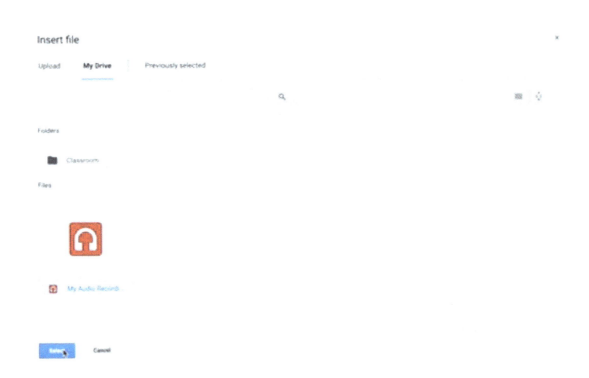

11. Once your file has been attached and you are done with the whole question, you can then proceed to go through your wok once again. The 'Back' option is for you to access previous pages in case you skipped some questions or you want to go through them for clarity sake. Once you are convinced with your work, you can then decide to submit by clicking on the 'Submit' option.

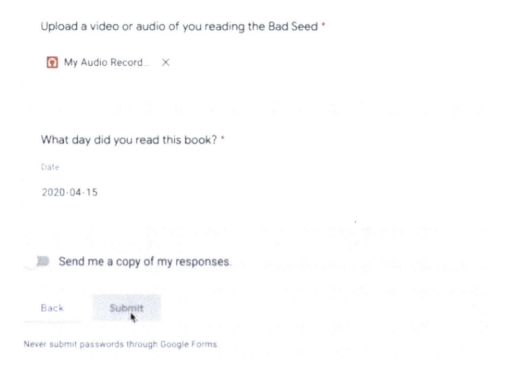

Upload a video or audio of you reading the Bad Seed *

⬙ My Audio Record...   ✕

What day did you read this book? *

Date

2020-04-15

▧   Send me a copy of my responses.

Back   Submit

Never submit passwords through Google Forms.

12. This then submits your assignments. As most quizzes are marked immediately, you can decide to check your score by clicking on the 'View score' option.

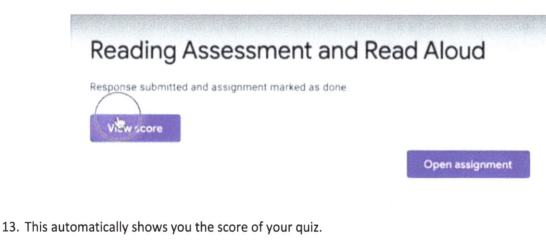

Reading Assessment and Read Aloud

Response submitted and assignment marked as done.

View score

Open assignment

13. This automatically shows you the score of your quiz.

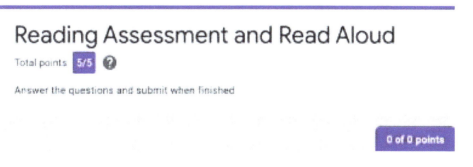

Reading Assessment and Read Aloud

Total points 5/5 ❓

Answer the questions and submit when finished

0 of 0 points

The quiz assignment however takes different forms such as:

1. The Multiple Choice Questions – These questions always have various options and will always include one correct answer. Answering these forms of questions requires you to click on the answer which you believe is the right one (or clicking on the circle of the answer).

2. The Short or Long Answer Questions – These questions always require you to input the answer in a box that will have been provided. These answers can either be short or long although the space provided by the box will always be sufficient for the answer required from you.

3. The Checkbox Questions – These questions provide small boxes that have to be checked or marked in front of these answers. Most of these questions however always require more than one answer hence you have to check the box with the answers that you think are right and then leave the others unchecked.

4. The Dropdown Questions –These questions usually do not have their options visible until you select the 'Choose' option which then reveals the various options after which you can select the one you deem correct.

5. The File Upload Question – These questions usually need you to upload your answers. You have to have saved your answer on your computer or Google Drive before you can then proceed to select the 'ADD FILE' option after which you can then click on the answer (file) and upload it to the question.

6. The Linear Scale Question – These questions are defined by numbers which scale up between two ends. For example selecting a 5 means you are very satisfied, while selecting a 3 means you are just satisfied while selecting a 1 means you are not satisfied at all.

How satisfied were you with the quality of the training guides?

	1	2	3	4	5	
Not at all satisfied	○	○	○	○	○	Very satisfied

7. There is also the Multiple Choice Grid Questions. These questions are similar to the Linear Scale Question but the only difference is that there are more than one linear scale in the Multiole Choice Grid Questions.

How much did you like each part of the conference?

	Strongly disliked	Disliked	Neither disliked nor liked	Liked	Strongly Liked
The instructors	○	○	○	○	○
The food	○	○	○	○	○
The training guides	○	○	○	○	○
The location	○	○	○	○	○
The online system	○	○	○	○	○

You can then check the circles based on how you felt for each part of the conference. You might have 'Strongly Liked' the instructors while you did not enjoy the location hence checking the circle for 'Strongly Disliked' the location.

8. The Checkbox Grid Question – This differs from the Multiple Choice Grid Question because the same answer can be chosen for a particular category in this question type. The answers on the left are selected in other to be in sync or correspond with the answers located at the top.

Select which forms of energy are renewable and which are non-renewable.

	Oil	Coal	Wind	Solar
Renewable	☐	☐	☐	☐
Non-renewable	☐	☐	☐	☐

Wind and Solar are renewable hence you have to check the box binding both options and then do the same for the non- renewable oil and coal.

9. The Date Questions – There are spaces provided with a particular format that shows what date you intend to fill in. The formats vary although the usual format as the month appearing first, followed by the date and then the year.

Date

mm/dd/yyyy

10. The Time Question – These questions require you to tell the time as an answer. There is the box where you fill in the time and also you can shuffle between the 'AM' and 'PM' options.

Google Classroom for Mobile Devices

Downloading the Application

1. You can download the application on your mobile phone app store if it is an iOS device or the play store if it is an android device.
2. Input the 'Google Classroom' into the search option and press enter to search. Proceed to download the 'Google classroom' application.
3. Select the 'Get Started' option located at the middle of the page.
4. You can proceed to sign in if you have an account but if not, you should create a new account.
5. Your personal information should then be entered in the necessary fields.

Profile Photo

1. There is the 'Menu' option located at the top of homepage. The 'Menu' option is represented by three horizontal lines.

2. You should then proceed to select the 'Settings' option.

3. Once you select the 'Account Settings', select the 'Update Photo' option and then proceed to click on the 'Set Profile Photo'.

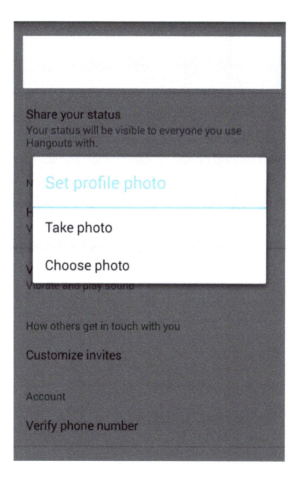

4. You can then decide to either select from your gallery by clicking on the 'choose from photos' or select the 'take a photo'.

Customizing Notifications

1. Select the 'Menu' option which is located at the top.

2. Select the 'Settings' option located on the dropped down Menu.

3. Navigate to the tab for notifications and select if you want to have the notifications on or off.

4. Selecting the 'Turn off' option for 'Receive email notifications' helps to have the notifications turned off. You can then select the 'Turn off' option for the 'Device Notifications' to have all your notifications turned off.

Joining a Class

You can join a class by either using the class code or by email invitation.

Using the Class Code

1. The Google Classroom app should be opened.
2. You should then select the '+' sign located at the top right of your classroom home page. You should then select the 'Join Class'.
3. Your teacher would then provide you with the class code which you should enter into the box provided.
4. Once you are done entering the code, you should then select the 'Join' option.

Using the Email invitation

1. Log in to your Google Mail app and check your inbox.
2. Your teacher will have sent an email to you hence you should search for the message having the subject: Class Invitation: '<CLASS NAME>'.

Select the 'Join' option in other to accept the invitation to the class.

Viewing your Class Resource Page

You must be on your classroom homepage in other to access this. The following steps will help you to access your class resource page:

1. Select the class you want to view.
2. Select the 'Menu' option found at the top left corner of the home page. The 'Menu' option is represented by 3 horizontal lines.

You will then be able to access a variety of class resources including: Classes – which helps you to access all the classes you are enrolled in, Calendar – which helps you to access the calendar of the assignments for your class and the due dates and the Classroom folders – which helps you to access the contents of the class including assignments, attachments and the teachers class folders.

Commenting on Class Announcement

1. Navigate to the Stream page by clicking on the 'Stream' option.
2. Once you do this, it is possible for a notification to appear centred at the top of your screen indicating a 'Stream was updated' caption. Proceed to select the 'Show' option which pops under the notification.
3. A post made to the class stream will appear at the middle of your screen. There will be a 'Add a class comment' box located under the post where you can then enter whatever comment you wish to make on the post.

4. Once your comment has been entered, you can then send your comment to be visible to other people in the class (both teacher and students) by clicking on the 'POST' option.

Accessing a Topic

1. There is an icon at the top right of your page which indicates the 'topic filter' option. Select this icon.
2. To access any topic, you should click on it so as to view it.

Posting an Announcement

1. Select the class you wish you make a post in.
2. There is a '+' sign located at the bottom right of your page, select the 'Create' option.

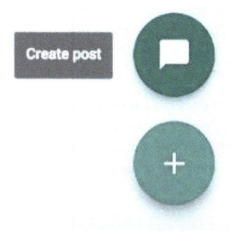

3. You can then input whatever message you want shared with the class in the 'Share with your class' box provided below.
4. Click on the 'POST; option so as to have your message posted to the class so they can all see it.

Attaching a file from your phone

1. There is the 'Attach' option represented by a paper clip icon, click on this icon.
2. You can then access the files on your phone by clicking on the 'Select files from your computer' option. Once the file has been found, you should then click on it. Make sure that your file is already saved on your phone however.
3. Select the 'Upload' option.

Attaching a file from Google Drive

1. This option is represented by the Google Drive icon. Select this icon in other to access the Google Drive.
2. Once the file has been found, click on the file and select the 'Add' option.

Attaching a YouTube Video

1. This option is represented by the YouTube icon. Select this icon so you can access YouTube.
2. You can then use the search bar to filter through till you find the video you want. Select the video once you are done and click on the 'Add' option.

Attaching a Link

1. This option is represented by the Link icon.
2. A box then appears in which you can have your linked pasted in it.
3. You should then select the 'ADD LINK' option.

Completing a PDF Assignment

1. Select the class where the assignment has been posted.
2. Once you find the assignment, you should then select the assignment title. It is possible for the assignment to be on the homepage of your class or located under a topic.
3. A new page is where you are then directed to. This page allows you to make comments on the posted assignment using the 'Add class comment' option, you can proceed to read the assignment, and you can also send your teacher a private comment using the 'Add a private comment; option.

In a situation where your assignment does not require you to have any work completed nor have any file attached and all you have to do is to view the contents of the PDF assignment, you can mark your assignment as completed by clicking on the 'MARK AS DONE' option. This pops up a box where you can select the ''MARK AS DONE' option in other for your assignment to be completed.

MARK AS DONE

Attaching a file that already exists

1. Select the 'ADD' option if you have a file that exists already and you want to have it attached to your video assignment. This 'ADD' option provides you with the following options:
    *   Google Drive - Select this if your already existing file has been saved in your Google Drive and you want to import it from here.
    *   Link – Select this if it is a link that you want to attach.
    *   File – Select this if the already existing file has been saved on your computer or personal device and you want to import it from here.

Select the 'TURN IN' option once you are sure that your submission has been attached. This then makes a box pop up asking you if you are sure about proceeding to have your work submitted. Select the 'TURN IN' option in other to have your assignment submitted.

Creating a New File to Complete your Submission

1. Select the 'CREATE' option in other to have a file created from the scratch on the Google Drive. This pops up a couple of options including: Documents, Slides, Sheets and Drawings.

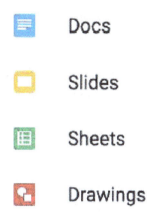

2. A file will be created for your submission once you have selected any of the options previously stated.

3. Select the file and tab that allows you to have the file edited and helps you to complete the assignment will be opened.

4. You can then proceed to click on the 'TURN IN' option located at the top right corner.
5. This then makes a box pop up asking you if you are sure about proceeding to have your work submitted. Select the 'TURN IN' option in other to have your assignment submitted.

Completing a Video Assignment

1. Select the class where the assignment has been posted.
2. Once you find the assignment, you should then select the assignment title. It is possible for the assignment to be on the homepage of your class or located under a topic.
3. A new page is where you are then directed to. This page allows you to make comments on the posted assignment using the 'Add class comment' option, you can proceed to read the assignment, and you can also send your teacher a private comment using the 'Add a private comment; option.

In a situation where your video assignment does not require you to have any work completed nor have any file attached and all you have to do is to view the contents of the video assignment, you can mark your assignment as completed by clicking on the 'MARK AS DONE' option. This pops up a box where you can select the ''MARK AS DONE' option in other for your video assignment to be completed.

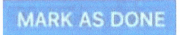

Attaching a file that already exists

1. Select the 'ADD' option if you have a file that exists already and you want to have it attached to your video assignment. This 'ADD' option provides you with the following options:
   - Google Drive - Select this if your already existing file has been saved in your Google Drive and you want to import it from here.
   - Link – Select this if it is a link that you want to attach.
   - File – Select this if the already existing file has been saved on your computer or personal device and you want to import it from here.

Select the 'TURN IN' option once you are sure that your submission has been attached.This then makes a box pop up asking you if you are sure about proceeding to have your work submitted. Select the 'TURN IN' option in other to have your assignment submitted.

Creating a New File to Complete your Submission

1. Select the 'CREATE' option in other to have a file created from the scratch on the Google Drive. This pops up a couple of options including: Documents, Slides, Sheets and Drawings.

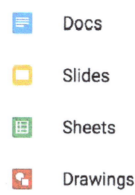

Docs

Slides

Sheets

Drawings

2. A file will be created for your submission once you have selected any of the options previously stated.

3. Select the file and tab that allows you to have the file edited and helps you to complete the assignment will be opened.

4. You can then proceed to click on the 'TURN IN' option located at the top right corner.
5. This then makes a box pop up asking you if you are sure about proceeding to have your work submitted. Select the 'TURN IN' option in other to have your assignment submitted.

Completing a Quiz

1. Navigate to the 'Stream' page as this where any quiz posted by your instructor will be found. If it is not located here, you should then check the 'Topic' page.
2. Select the 'Menu' option represented by three horizontal lines. This 'Menu' option allows you to be able to access the quiz.
3. Once you have completed the quiz, you can then select the 'SUBMIT' option.

Basic Functions

These are basic functions that you should be aware of when using the Google Classroom app on your mobile devices (iOS or Android). They include:

1. Select any class you want to access.

2. This then opens up 3 tabs at the top of your screen page: the STREAM tab, the CLASSMATES tabs and the ABOUT tab. The STREAM tab gives you access to view the class homepage, the CLASSMATES tab gives you access to the lists of the students in the class while the ABOUT tab introduces you to the description of the class.

3. Select the 'Menu' option located at the top left corner of your screen. This then pops up a couple of options for your Google Classroom interaction. The options include: Classes, Calendar and Classroom folders. The 'Classes' options gives you access to go back to the Google Classroom homepage and from there you can have access to all of your classes. The Calendar lets you access a calendar of assignments on your Google Calendar. Your Classroom folder allows you to access the contents of the class.

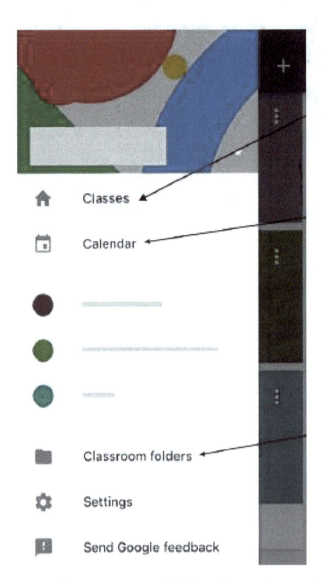

4. This sidebar also allows you to have access to all of the classes that you have enrolled in and your account settings.

CHAPTER FIVE

GOOLE CLASSROOM EXTENSION AND APPS

There are a lot of applications and extensions that work with the Google Classroom. These interactions with other apps and the Google Classroom help the teachers and students to save time and share information between the Classroom and the apps with ease. This list helps you to explore apps and extensions that you might be aware of already or new apps that you have not seen. They include:

1. Share to Classroom – This is an extension that lets web pages be shared easily to your classrooms so that your students can easily access them. Your students can be directed to the right page that you want them on at such a quick time and it is always reliable when you use this extension. This extension is designed by Google and is totally free to everyone. Posts, announcements, assignments, web pages can be created and saved so as to have them posted on the Google Classroom later.

2. Kami – This is also an extension and DriveApp and is effective for interpreting PDF files and documents. This is highly recommended for editing PDF files. Some of the features can be used for free and it combines wonderfully with the Google Classroom.

3. Mote Voice Commenting – This is a Google extension which serves the purpose of making voice comments on Google Docs, Google Slides and Google Sheets. This also combines well with the Google Classroom. Mote has a wide range of languages it can transcribe to (more than 15 languages including the well spoken ones English, French, Spanish, German and Mandarin Chinese). This is also effective in questioning students and also making comments or feedbacks.

4. Classwork Zoom for Google Classroom – This extension helps to visualize data from history data to a timeline which can be analyzed faster and with more ease. This extension however is not in any way related to the popular ZOOM app for video conferencing.

5. Insert Learning – This Google extension allows your websites to be turned into interactive sessions and helps you to perfectly blend your lesson plans. Insert Learning can make an interactive lesson from any webpage available. It was created to help students get more learning experience and it sure serves the purpose.

6. Squigl – This app helps to catch the attention of students for a longer period of time by turning or transforming the class materials into other learning methods that are effective.

7. Writable – this app is dedicated to developing great writers by providing assignments that can be customized and also integrates very well with the Google Classroom. This app also helps the teachers to motivate students to develop interests and lead them towards the path of becoming proficient writer with purpose. Schools can also access and have their writing growth monitored through this app.

8. codeHS – This app helps to introduce your students to the coding world. This app contains a platform for teaching that is comprehensive, includes a web- based curriculum, tools and resources for the teacher and also provides opportunity for developing professionally.

9. PBS –This app makes use of resources that are ready for the classroom (thousands of them) in other to spark a sense of curiosity in students and reach the set goals of the curriculum. These resources are also designed to conform to the standards of both the nation and the state.

10. Studytracks – This app drives the engagement of the student by reforming your curriculum and making music from it. This helps to get your students engaged, retentive and help them achieve more while in the classroom or out of it.

11. Pearson Education – This app is designed to have contents, rosters and assessments shared with the G Suite for education as it integrates with it. This app works with single sign- on access.

12. ASSISTments – This free online tool can simultaneously send feedbacks to both the students and the teacher once the assignment has been completed. This app is majorly for assignments and assessments dealing with mathematics.

13. Additio App – This app helps the teacher to have the classroom day- to- day activities, interactions and planning of lessons to run with total ease. This app also serves as a classroom planner and a digital gradebook and helps to have the progress of your students monitored and tracked.

14. Aeries – This app makes use of data management software solutions that help your curriculum to be enhanced. The app also lets you have new classes created, have the students' scores imported and other functions.

15. Aeries Student Information System – This is an app and extension platform that allows the grades, scores of tests, attendance of your student to be effectively managed and tracked. This also lets these details of the students to be shared with both parents and students with ease.

16. DuoLingo – This app and extension is viewed as the most ideal classroom companion to learn languages by many around the world. DuoLingo lets each student have access to personalized practices and feedbacks and also ensures the student's get the best from the classroom.

17. Edmodo – This is an app that is great for learning done over long distances and hybrid. It allows effective sharing of materials and messages, and can also be accessible at any point in time or place. This app brings together all the tools necessary in your classroom as it also aids easy communications and management of the contents in your class.

18. Desmos – This app is great for calculations and making graphs that are elegant and also stimulators in maths. The app serves a wide range of purposes such as serving as a calculator, creating presentation images having high quality. The app is also exceptional for activities in the classroom as Desmos aids in having mathematical concepts connected to concrete by the students.

19. Edpuzzle – This app allows you to create any video of your lesson. You can aid the understanding of your student by making videos and editing it to suit your students. All of the courses in the Classroom and students can be imported automatically once the teacher is signed up due to the integration of the Edpuzzle.

20. LearnZillion – This is an extension that provides a platform containing a large library of math and language lessons of art that are interactive, quizzes, assessments, assignments and videos for your students. The app also provides the feature of having the progress of your students tracked, their achievements on the assessments and assignments and has the results reported to the dashboard of the teacher for further assessment.

21. Nearpod – This is a tool that helps with interactions an assessments and serves the classroom very well as it provides effects that are amazing. The concept of the app is really simple. Presentations can be designed by the teachers and such presentations can include Polls, videos, images, boards for drawing, web content etc.

22. PBS Learning Media – This is an app and is great for accessing digital resources that are ready for the classroom and targeted in sync with the curriculum. These digital resources are available in their thousands on this. The PBS Learning Media makes use of the public media and helps to make the achievements of students and effectiveness of the teacher better. The resources always meet the standards at national level and have audios, interactive videos, documents and in- depth lesson plans. To find what you need, you can have them filtered by levels of grade, subjects, standards and special collections. Resources can also be shared with your colleagues or added to your 'Favourites' so you can always access them with ease.

23. BookWidgets – This is an online platform that also helps to have interactive quizzes that are personalized for your classroom rather than the usual tests done on paper. These exercises on the BookWidgets platform are always graded automatically once you have submitted. This provides the teacher with enough time to provide timely feedbacks to the student without having to stress as this can be done with just a click. This platform also ensures that information needed to help you identify the areas where your students are experiencing problems is quickly brought to your attention so you can sort it out. This platform also provides a real- time tracking of the progress of your students anytime they are using the BookWidgets platform either at home or in the classroom.

24. IXL – This is a platform that gives you access to practice a lot of topics (over 7000) including topics in maths, sciences, social studies, language arts and Spanish. The practice offered on this platform is unlimited. Students who use this platform are always motivated by awards and certificates which are presented to them when they have successfully dealt with the interactive questions provided by the platform.

25. Read & Write for Google Chrome – This platform is very easy to use and the intuition is so wonderful. Read & Write for Google Chrome gives access to help you create your own documents, web pages and other documents found in your Google Drive (such as Google Docs, Google Sheets, Google Slides, PDFs and ePubs among others). These documents are always very accessible on this platform. This platform does not require so much learning abilities and style has it has been designed to meet everyone's needs as the digital contents are suitable for everyone.

Google Classroom Extra Features

This section introduces you to a couple for extra features that the Google Classroom provides. They include:

1. Virtual Office Hours – The 'About' tab located at the top of the Google Classroom homepage helps the teacher to have links and resources posted so that it can be accessed by students all school year round. Virtual Office Hours is made available to the students when the teacher has the permalink of the Google Hangout copied and then linked to the 'About' page of the Google Classroom. This makes the students and teachers to be able to communicate in a chat by selecting the link provided by the teacher on the 'About' page. This can however be done during the office hours.

2. Virtual Faculty Meetings – Meetings are one of the important daily activities of teachers and is usually time consuming. Google Classroom provides the faculty with the possibility of having the meetings reduce. The faculty can join the Google Classroom as suggested by the administrator of the school. In order to have the faculty meetings facilitated by a flipped approach, the Google Classroom can then be linked with short videos. To enable data to be provided by teachers, they can be provided with forms

for them to attend to or even polled questions for them to answer. The stream also allows different news to be shared by the various departments in the faculty.

3. PLCs (Collaboration with Peers) – There is a '+' option located at the top right corner of your Google Classroom homepage which allows teachers to join a classroom as students. Teachers can proceed to join the classroom by selecting the 'Join Class' option and then enter the class code of the PLC classroom that must have been set up. The created PLC Classroom allows the teachers to share documents, data and meeting notes. The 'TURN IN' option located in the classroom also allows the teachers to have the results of their classroom from projects or assignments to be submitted. For Professional Developments, just like students, teachers can proceed to join a Google Classroom. The Google Classroom 'Stream' tab allows materials, activities and resources for the Professional Development to be organized. The resources for the Professional Development class can then be accessed with ease by the teachers.

4. Observing other Classrooms – The Google Classroom offers teachers to improve their practice by collaborating with one another. The Google Classroom also allows for the enrolment of other teachers or administrators as students in a particular classroom. This can be done by joining the class the usual way by entering the class code. The teachers who just joined the class then turn to observers and notice what best practices and assignment types are put in use. This can however be done when the teachers are all in the same domain. Teachers can then collaborate across different classrooms and also helps them to work with their mentors.

5. Google Drive as One Storage – The Google Drive provides a system for automatic management and organization in the Google Classroom. All Google Classroom documents or files that have been submitted by the students are saved as an automatic file system in the Google Drive. This serves as one storage because all the files are saved here and thus makes it a central location for all the works of the students. If the works of the students are done on another program, they can proceed to take screenshots of the work and have it submitted to the Google Classroom as screenshots. There is the 'Upload File' option located on the page for assignment submission on the Google Classroom and this helps the students to submit the screenshots of their work. The submitted screenshots of the work are also saved to the Google Drive folder of the Google Classroom.

6. Less Cheating – Only the teacher can access the folder containing the assignments of the Google Classroom hence students do not have access to this. The class documents are not present in a shared folder hence it is impossible for the works of other students to be copied by any of them. Having a Google Drive folder to be shared with the whole class enables the students to be able to view each other's works hence the possibility of copying and an increase in cheating however there is an upgrade from simply having to use the Google Drive. The teacher can also find out a work has been edited or by who by using the revision history. This can be done by accessing the work of each student. Revisions are always recorded at frequent intervals and once it is observed that there is only one revision for a particular student, then chances are the document was copied from another student.

7. Making Polls – In a situation where the amount of students who want to attend an event is to be known, it is possible to create an assignment to find out. For students who want to attend the event, the students are to select the 'MARK AS DONE' option whereas the ones who are not attending should not respond at all. This then enables the teacher to have a list identifying those who want to attend and those who are not attending by the 'Done' and 'NOT DONE' options located in front of the assignment. This is however not available if you are using Google Forms.

8. Simplified Turn In – It is not uncommon to have students not remember to have their assignments turned in or have their sharing settings changed when making use of the Google Docs. Once they make this mistake, the assignments cannot be accessed or viewed by the teachers. This issues has however been eliminated by the Google Classroom as the documents are immediately saved in the Google Drive of both the teachers and the students. This Google Drive allows the document to be accessed by both the teachers and the students. The 'TURN IN' option provided by the Google Classroom serves as a signal that the students are ready to have their work accessed and the teacher is notified. Students are in charge of the ownership of the work when they are answering it but once they click on the 'TURN IN' option, they have automatically transferred the ownership of the document to the teacher. Once the work has been submitted to the teacher, the students do not have the option to make changes or edits to the work anymore although they can still open the assignment to view it.

9. Allows Collaboration – The Google Classroom encourages collaboration between students in the classroom. The teacher can choose how the assignments can be viewed when creating assignments by selecting either 'View Only' or to allow students to be able to make edits. If the teacher selects the 'Students can edit file' option, it means the document can be edited by all of the students hence the students can contribute to a class activity or project. In case you want to enhance collaboration in the class, Google Slides and Google Sheets are great tools for that. Students can work on individual slides on a Google Slides presentation. Students can also write on separate cells on the same Google Sheets. These tools are very great for crowd- sourcing data and information. Students can also work on separate individual tabs on the Google Sheet. All of the works of the students can be reviewed in one single document.

10. Watch Students Do Homework – It is possible for the assignments to be submitted at any time of the day or week since the students can access the Google Classroom on the web. Students work submitted at any time of the 24 hours in a day can be observed by the teacher. Documents which are been worked on by the students can also be accessed by the teacher to monitor their progress. This feature provides the possibility of real- time feedbacks and interactions as the Google Drive can be accessed by the teacher and students working after school hours can be seen in the assignment folder.

Google Classroom: Pros and Cons

Just like everything we are familiar with, the Google Classroom has pros and cons concerned with making use of it. This section gives you an insight into this.

PROS

1. Communication and Sharing: The Google classroom provides an effective platform for this. One of the best things about using the Google Classroom is the Google Docs. The Google Docs can be accessed at once by the students through their Google Drive once a post or assignment has been created and shared with them since they are saved online. The Google Drive folders offer the features of Google Docs to be organized and customized with ease. Emails are then no longer necessary when information is to be shared as information can be passed by simply having a document created and made available to as much people as desired.

2. Accessibility and Ease of Use: Accessing Google Classroom is not an issue even for non Google users. Although the Google Classroom is accessed from the Google Chrome browser available on computers

and mobile devices (iOS and Android), it also ensures adding multiple students is easy, Google documents can be designed for assignments and announcements, YouTube videos can be posted, links added or Google Drive files attached. Log in for students is easy and the process of having assignments received, completed and turned in is easy.

3. Assignment Process: The Google Classroom makes sure that the process of creating and sharing an assignment is easy and sped up. This also applies to when students receive and turn in their assignments with such speed too. The process of creating, sharing, receiving and turning in assignments is so speedy and fast when using the Google Classroom. Feedbacks can be offered immediately, students can be monitored to find out which of them have turned in their assignments or not.

4. Effective Feedbacks: The Google Classroom provides you with a platform to give support to your online students immediately. Feedbacks are more effective this way as they become comments freshly made and this leaves a big impact on the mind of those receiving the feedbacks.

5. Paperless: We are gradually moving to the era when papers will be a thing of the past. Google Classroom is definitely a big leap towards that moment. All of your materials and resources are centralized in a cloud- based location (the Google Drive) and there is no need to have to print on paper or even having your work lost or damaged.

6. For all and sundry: Asides from teachers and students using the Google Classroom, other people with interest in education and learning can make use of the platform. Colleagues from a work place can all use the Google Classroom for meetings, sharing information or development on professional basis.

7. Easy Commenting: The Google Classroom provides a great deal of sections for both teachers and students to make comments. URLs can also be created for comments of interests and can be used when further discussions are made online.

8. User- Friendly: The Google Classroom provides an online platform with simple design with details which are user- friendly and intuitive, The Google Classroom helps you to feel at home even when you are using it for the first time.

CONS

1. Account Management Difficulty: You cannot use multiple domains to access the Google Classroom. Also it is not advisable to use your personal Google account due to restrictions hence the need to make use of G Suite for Education. Once you already have a personal Google account, juggling the multiple accounts will definitely be cumbersome. For instance, if there is a photo that you want to post in the Google Classroom and it is on your personal Google account, you cannot just post it like that. You have to save it on the hard drive of your computer, log out, use your Google Classroom account to log in again and then upload it.

2. 'Googlish': The icons in the Google Classroom are basically icons used on Google hence only Google users might be able to interact easily unlike the new non Google users. Although Google and YouTube are integrated together when you want to share file, some other tools which are popular are not incorporated in the Google Classroom. The Google Classroom will although be enjoyable if all the tools you are going to use are incorporated with Google services.

3. Update: The feeds on the Google Classroom homepage does not automatically update. This leaves learners with the task of having to refresh at random so as to be able to view recent announcements that may be important.

4. Automated Quizzes and Tests: The Google Classroom does not have all the features to totally replace the Learning Management System due to the fact that there are not automated quizzes or test. Unlike other the Learning Management Systems, the Google Classroom does not provide automated quizzes for the students. The Google Classroom is however more of an experience for learning than an online program that is fully run.

5. Impersonal: Google Classroom does not create such a learning environment that is well blended as there is no integration between the Google Classroom and the Google Hangout yet. This makes interactions and sharing of documents or messages between the students and the teachers to be limited to only Google documents. Interactions and relationships built between the students and the teachers is key to effectively interacting in the classroom and this can be brought about by creating online discussions. However, the Google Classroom does not have a feature for the live chat yet.

Managing your Classroom

It is essential for your classroom to be able to provide access to all students without prejudice (equal access), enhance communication and collaboration among students and also invoke their creative spirit and critical thinking even though it is an online classroom. There should also make available room for differentiation so that all students need can be met, active learning is also encouraged along with an increase in the level of engagements of the students. Tools are provided to the teachers by the Google classroom in other to ease these managements.

- Communication and Collaboration – There are tools provided by the Google Classroom that help teachers and students to communicate with each other at all times. There is a Gmail app that has been integrated with the Google Classroom hence mails can be sent and received by both the students and the teachers. Posts made on the 'Stream' tab in the Google Classroom also serves as a means of communicating along with private comment option available under assignments and also the grading tool lets the teacher to make comment on works submitted by the student.
Collaboration is also very well achievable in the Google Classroom. Teachers and peers can have open conversations on the 'Stream' tab in the Google Classroom. Teachers can also create group assignments and share them with the students while asking them to work together and this allows them to interact well with one another.

- Active Engagement and Active Learning – The Google Classroom will not be effective or efficient if active learning and engagement does not take place. It is the task of the teacher to make sure that strategies are put in place to ensure there is an increase in student ownership in learning although the students may make claim that they are at a comfortable level with using technology. Getting the students engaged in the classroom is easy as there are several interactive methods put in place in the Google Classroom. The Google Classroom lets links, videos, games which are interactive and corroborative assignments (full of lesson and assignments) be included and added to the class by the teachers. The previously mentioned apps and extensions also makes a limitless range of possible engagements in the Google Classrooms. These apps are easily integrated with the Google Classroom hence very compatible. The 'Share to Classroom extension' for Google Chrome makes it easy for almost all websites to be shared to the Google Classroom.

- Differentiation – Differentiation of assignments and tasks in the Google Classroom is simply a breeze. Lessons can be assigned to the whole class, students on individual basis or a group of particular students. This can be done on the 'Classwork' tab of the Google Classroom. Google Classroom helps to eliminate the time consuming and very stressful task of having assignments or lessons assigned to students on by on in the classroom. Once the assignments have been created by the teacher, the teacher can proceed to select the students who are to receive the assignments by clicking on the checkbox in front of the names of the students and then proceed to send. This can also be done for a group or other people.

- Assessment and Feedback – Having the students assessed and feedbacks provided is a way of managing your Google Classroom and can be done in a couple of ways. Google forms can be created as a quiz by the teacher to test for understanding. The Google forms are graded automatically upon submission and the Classroom is where the results are sent to and stored. For data analysis, the results are then exported to Google Sheets. Questions that are thought provoking or exit tickets can be created by using the question feature when an assignment is to be created. This can be done by the teacher. The Classroom grading tool is also a method which helps the teacher to have the work of the students assessed, comments can also be made on the works and once the assignments have been graded, the grading tool helps to return it to the students with feedbacks included.

- Strength of Students – This is effective in managing your class effectively. You should post random questions or quotes which do not have to relate to the class but can help to channel the inner being of your students into being awakened. There is a culture of positive values and acceptance that is built when you know the strength of your students and work on them. Your students are then confident in their abilities when you do this. When faced with obstacles in the class, your students will then be confident and know that the obstacles are things that can be overcome and worked through. Once you start and work on the strength of your students, you can then manage your class effectively.

- Information and Skills – Nothing can be more confusing to students in the Google Classroom than when they do not have the proper information and skills to aid them. If an assignment has been given, it is imperative for you to teach them how to access the contents that you are teaching. Students should be taught about how they can obtain new information, how they can study for tests, how they should manage their time and also organize themselves. It is important to have the students empowered with skills which are effective and efficient for exploring the contents that they are expected to know and also include study skills.

- Green Zone – This indicates that your students should be comfortable when they are in your class. You do not have to be the goofy teacher, but it is important to put your students at ease before learning takes place. You can engage them in riddles, trivia or short jokes just to make the class at ease. These few minutes of making your students relax should be at the beginning of the class as this helps your students to relax and then flow with you in the class.

- Organize Content –The contents in your Google Classroom should be properly organized. You can go ahead and organize them according to folders such as topic, month or subject as this makes accessing such contents very easy. The Google Drive provides you with enough things to be assigned in your Google Classroom. Running your class will be such an easy process once you have properly organized your content.

- Clean Google Classroom Feed – Once multiple tasks are assigned regularly in the classroom, the feed becomes untidy because it has been very busy. In a bid to keep your feed clean and ensure easy navigation, you can have older assignments deleted. Assignments that are still in use should however be left alone as you can always want to recall them. Cleaning your feed is however a a personal choice of the teacher. You should have the assignments properly arranged in case you want to refer to previous assignments.

Tips for Using the Google Classroom

1. To put relevant older materials at the top in a bid to get the attention of the students, make use of the 'move to top' option - Assignments, questions or announcements are bumped to the top of your class stream by using the move to top option. In case your students have not turned in your assignment or there is an upcoming deadline that you want to remind your students about, you can decide to use this option.

2. 'Students' tab allows you to send a mail to everyone in a class – Once you are on the 'Students' tab, select the checkbox located at the top of all of your students and this helps you to select every one of the student. You can then proceed to click on the 'Actions' options and then the 'Email' option and this helps you to get the attention of all the students to whatever it is you are sharing with them.

3. Comments should be properly used – Students in the Google Classroom can receive different types of comments from the teacher. It is important to know when to use each of them.
    - Add class comment – This adds comments under a post or assignment in the class stream. This comment is then visible to everyone enrolled in the class. These kind of comments are suitable for sharing comments that would benefit all of the class.
    - Add private comments – This only happens when you have selected a particular student. This comment bar is for making comments that is only visible to the student and is always found under a student's submitted assignment.
    - Add comments in a document or slide or sheet or drawing – This can be done only when you have selected the file of the student that has been submitted. Once you have highlighted what you want to pass a comment on, select the black speech bubble icon as the specific comment is attached to the highlighted item.

4. Share 'right now' links with assignments – Contents can be placed in the classroom stream by announcements without having an assignment created for the students to submit. Students can then be provided with links, documents or files and videos that are important to them.

5. Replace the mouse with the keyboard – The moving of the mouse is not as effective as the clicking of the keyboard. This is more effective when making use of the Google classroom. Grades can be easily entered in the Google Classroom by pressing the key with the arrow down icon in order to move on to the next student. Names of students can be cycled around by using the arrow keys rather than the mouse.

6. Email Tips-If you have older students, you should make use of the email feature.For the younger grades, this is not a feature you should take interest in. Once a student has their assignment marked as 'done', you should make up your mind on the notifications sent to your mail. Your email inbox will be a mess if you get notified once every student in a class of 20-25 students mark their assignment as done. Select the 'Menu' icon (represented by 3 horizontal lines) located at the top left corner of your Google

Classroom homepage. Click on the 'Settings' option located at the bottom and then your email preference can be marked in the checkbox.

7. Online Discussion Tips-Discussions about assignments can be started in the Google Classroom as it has the feature that supports this. The interface works just like a window for chatting or a forum. This feature can be made available to the students or included in a project for collaboration on their part. A lesson on the expectations of the classroom and digital citizenship should be taught before you take the step previously mentioned. Once it is noticed that the students are using the platform for purposes asides the topic or educational topics and rambling about topics which do not concern the class, you can withdraw the discussion privilege and have the discussions muted.

8. Grading Tips –Your online grading platform may be integrated with your Google Classroom or not. You should make serious findings about what options are available for your project. You can work with this program by having your grade book program reduced to half of your screen and also have your grade list on your Google Classroom reduced to half of the other side of your screen. Once the grade book program and the Google Classroom grade books are placed side by side on your screen, you can then glance at the grade list and have the grades added to the grading program.

9. Keyboard Shortcut Tips - Your students should be taught about the magic of knowing keyboard commands. Imagine a student who has been typing for a long time and they mistakenly have the whole page deleted; the panic and horror written on their face. Now imagine he joy on their face when you just select the 'undo' button or click on control Z. You should teach your students the keyboard shortcuts as this is really important and will help them when working in the Google Classroom. The sooner your students learn the shortcuts, the better for them because their digital careers will need the knowledge. Keyboard strokes are more effective when compared to the dragging of mouse.

10. Each assignment with attached template document – There are a couple of teachers that make sure that a template or a Google Document that is blank is attached to each assignment. This serves as a copy for each student. Google Classroom allows you to access the page of the assignment and view each student's thumbnail. A glance at this shows you if there has been progress or not. In a situation where there is no template available, you can have a blank Google document saved and then attach it to the assignment so as to be able to have a view of the thumbnail.

11. Demonstrate with a demo account – As a teacher, you cannot view your class as a student as the Google Classroom does not provide this feature yet. In other to access your class as a student, you have to create a student account. An alternative to this is to create a demo account and enrol as a student in other to have an experience of what a student account in the Google classroom is like and then demonstrate to your students.

12. Numbering Assignments – This is a very great tip for teachers. In fact, it is also a great tip for the students too. Asides from having your Google Drive orderly and tidy, it also helps to keep your classroom organized. This is also helpful in keeping a track of your assignments as all your assignments are numbered. This helps the students to know which assignment is due and which number is to come next.

13. Unsubmit Work - As much as you might think this is unnecessary, this always comes in handy in some situations. In a situation where the file you submitted is not for the assignment, you would then have to unsubmit. This is possible because the Google Classroom entails you having to deal with a lot of files hence it is possible to make a mistake and have files mixed up. Select the submitted assignment and the 'Unsubmit' option will become visible. You should then click on the 'Unsubmit' option so as to unsubmit.

14. Unenroll Class – It is possible that at the end of the term or year, you might want to leave the class since you are done. A student in Google Classroom can proceed to unenroll from a class once they want to. Select the 3- dotted icon located at the top of the screen once you select the class you want to leave. Click on the 'Unenroll' option so as to unenroll from the class.

15. Projects as Smaller Assignments – You can proceed to have your projects broken into smaller assignments so that you can have due dates attached to each assignments separately. It is necessary to consider alternative ways of having project- based learning implemented in the Google Classrooms as they (project- based learning) are of great importance and there is the need to leave behind the static one and done assignments. Students can be unnecessarily overwhelmed with big projects most especially students who have a hard time with time management. The projects should then be broken down into smaller assignments and due dates be attached to them for efficiency purposes.

Problems that Might Arise With Using the Goole Classroom

It is not uncommon to experience problems when using the Google Classroom hence this section gives you an insight into what problems you can experience and how to solve them.

1. Troubleshooting – This can happen when your classroom has a display showing 'Imported by...' when you are trying to import your Google classroom but then it is missing from the classroom. This problem can be resolved by you although it is necessary to make use of your personal or desktop computer.
   a. Create a new tab and navigate to the page where the trouble is.
   b. Proceed to have access your web browser Developer Tools. In case you do not know how to do this, press the Control + Shift + J for windows laptop and if you are using a Mac to do this, press Command + Shift + J.
   c. If this does not work, navigate to the page and click on the 'Remove' option.
   d. Once you can access the Developer Tools, click on the 'Console' tab.
   e. Scroll down while looking for any text written in red. The red text is an indication of the errors present on the page.
   f. If you do not want to use this process, navigate to your developer console and input the network tab in the search bar. Check out for any red text once on this page too as the red texts are an indication that the file needs to be worked on by *reading.com* as the files have not been successfully downloaded by the computer.

   The red texts are also an indication that the school or your district has made sure other resources or sites which host trusted and professional websites have been blocked and this causes a problem. The blocked network resources are then indicated by all of these errors.

2. Connection problems – Your Google Classroom might not function very well if your browser has the pop- up disabled. This is also indicated by a red message and shows that your Google Classroom is not well connected. Once you are connected to the Google Classroom, it is important for you to have the pop- up enabled for proper functioning.
   a. Once the pop- up has been disabled on the Goole Chrome, a picture appears at the top right corner of your search bar and you can change this in two ways.

- You can click on the picture that has appeared and then select the 'Always allow pop- ups' option.
- You can also click on the green lock also located at the top left and then click on the 'Give permission' option.

b. You should then proceed to log out. Once you are logged out, you should then log back in.

c. Select the 'Permission' tab. You should then click on the 'Allow' option as this enables both you and the students to have access to the contents and assignments from the dashboard.

3. Browser Issues – This can be fixed by having an full- fledged refrigerator applied to the Google Classroom site. If you do not know how to do this, press the CTRL and f5 keys on your browser at the same time. You can decide to use your favourite browser in any of the Firefox, Chrome or Explorer browsers. You should then proceed to have the cash and cookies cleared on your desired browser to ensure that the web page version you are on is the current one.

4. DNS's Problems – The DNS means Domain Name System and helps to have an IP address with words identified and it is remembered with ease as the website phone box. Your ISP (Internet Service Provider) provides this service. The steps include:

a. Proceed to have your local DNS case cleared in other to ensure that the latest ISP case has been caught.

b. Follow this command accordingly; Start > Command Prompt >>Type "ipconfig/flushdns" and then press the 'Enter' button. For details, select your operating system.

It is more effective to make use of an alternative DNS service rather than your ISPs if you have the chance of having access to a 3G network or a website if it still is not working on your personal computer. There are free public DNA services such as OpenDNS and Google Public DNS which are great for your use and available for you.

5. Students not syncing – This can happen in two different ways when the classroom has been imported: some of the students are not syncing and all of the students are not syncing.

a. When some of the students are not syncing – The first solution to this is to have your account reconnected with Google. This can be done through the following steps:

Step 1

1. Select the 'My Account' option located under your profile avatar (located in the top right corner of your Google Classroom home page).

2. Click on the 'Account Settings' option and this opens up further options.

3. Select the 'Google Classroom' option and then click in the 'Reconnect Google Account' option. Input *chrome//restart* in your URL bar and proceed.

Step2

At this point, it is important to make sure the students who are not syncing have accepted the Google Classroom invite sent to their mails. If students have not accepted, there is no way the students can be synced. There will be a greyed out section on the name of some students with 'invited' written in front of their names. These students are the ones who are pending and have not been synced. As soon as the students have accepted their invitations, proceed to select the 'Sync Students From Google' option in other to have the students synced. This can be done on the 'People' tab available on your Google Classroom page.

b. When all of the students are not syncing – This will most likely be as a result of the number of students in your class. The GoGuardian classroom allows a maximum of 115 students in a particular class. In an attempt to sync all the students in a class having more than 115 students, it is just right for the sync to fail. You should then proceed to have your class divided into smaller classrooms having not more than 115 students. You can then proceed to sync all of the students in the smaller class.

6. Turn In button redirects – This is a problem that students face when they try to have their assignments turned in and the 'Turn In' button redirects them to a Google Classroom block page. This can be as a reason of having your Scene to not include the *Google.com* as an added site to be allowed in the Scene and then having the Scene set to Block Mode. This allows the 'Turn In' option to redirect them automatically through *Google.com.* The solution to this is to have your Scene include an added URL as an   exception.   The   URL   to   be   added   to   the   exception   list   is *www.google.com/url?q=https%3A%2F%2Fclassroom.google.com*.* The URL include the *.

7. File Not Found – It is possible that when you click on an assignment or material that a 'File Not Found' error pops up or in a bid to have a photo or document attached, a progress bar that never gets completed in having the documents finally attached pops up or nothing at all. The solution to this however is not because you have done anything wrong as the most likely reason for this is that the Google Classroom is overloaded. This might be as a result of a lot of users logged on to the Google Classroom at that particular moment and the best thing you can do is to be patient and most like give it a trial later. It is then important for the teacher to relax on the due date or time and this also makes it reasonable not to keep doing your assignments till when it is almost close to the due date or time.

Frequently Asked Questions While Using the Google Classroom

Question: While using the Google Classroom, before I can see deadlines for each assignment, I have to open each subject before the due date can be visible. Is it possible to view all of the deadlines from the homepage without having to undertake the long process of viewing each assignment one by one?

Answer: You can access all of the due assignments at once. In other to be able to view all of the new assignments for all of your classes and the dates in which they will be due, click on the 'Menu' button (represented by 3 horizontal lines) located at the top left corner of your Google Classroom homepage. Go ahead to select the 'To-Do' option and it automatically reveals all of the due assignments and classes at once. Selecting the 'All Classes' option located at the top helps you to filter a couple of particular classes in your classroom.

Question: Is it possible to have works you have done previously moved or archived into your topic folders?

Answer: Your most recent topics can be moved to the top for your students to be able to access easily if only you are making use of Topics in the tab 'Classwork'. Topics and assignments cannot really be archived however you can decide to have a new topic created and have it named 'Archive'. Any assignment that is to be moved to the folder 'Archive' can then be selected by editing through the 3 dots located in front of the selected assignment. You can then replace the topic it is in with Archive. Archived topics cannot be organized into folders as it still will not be made accessible to the students hence they are at a disadvantage when this is done.

Topics should rather be reordered rather than doing that. There are various ways of having your topics ordered and organized either by Units or Weekly.

Question: As a regular company and not a school, can Google Classroom be used as a tool for classes that are paid for? Is that okay and possible?

Answer: This is okay and possible. A good number of people always use the Google Classroom as a tool to make others have access to contents and services which they provide. There is no known restriction on this as the Google Classroom is available to people who use Gmail.

Question: How do students get to complete an assignment that has a worksheet attached to them?

Answer: It is possible to make an extra copy of the assignment for each of your students if the attached worksheet is a Google Document. Once you make this possible, each student will have access to an individual copy and this copy is what can be shared between the teacher and the students. Once the students are done with their assignments and ready to copy, they would select the 'Turn In' option and then to see their submission, all the teacher has to do is to select the assignment.

Question: Once students have their assignments turned in, it is observed that there are coloured wedges (white, blue, grey or red) at the bottom of the work of the students and why does this happens?

Answer: This is actually not an issue. The colours basically just signify the types of document that have been submitted. A document with green wedge would signify Google Sheets, while one with blue wedge would signify Google Doc and another with orange wedge will signify Google Slides and so on.

Question: Once an assignment has been pushed out, is it possible to change the assignment to a question or change a question to an assignment?

Answer: There is no way to achieve this. Once an assignment is already posted, it cannot be changed back to a question. The only thing that can be done is to have the assignment deleted and then have a new one pushed out.

Question: Does Google Classroom monitor each student's activity in the classroom? Activities like how long a student has been logged in the classroom or the amount of people logged in at a particular time?

Answer: The Google Classroom does not have this feature added yet. It can only inform the teacher of how well a student has turned in their assignments for a given class.

Question: For courses and contents included upon creating a Google Classroom, do I own the intellectual right to my contents or Google?

Answer: Once you have created the Google Classroom, all of your content belongs to you. Google has only provided a platform for you to interact with your students; however you have the sole right to all of your contents and can decide to remove them from the Google Classroom unto any other platform of your choice.

Question: Can teachers make use of the Google Classroom to make live classes just like the Zoom app?

Answer: This is not possible. The Google Classroom does not support the live feature however teachers can only leave assignments for the students who get notified immediately and can then have access to the assignments.

Question: Can teachers make extra copies of created assignment materials in their Google Classroom?

Answer: It is possible to create extra copies of assignments when using the Google Classroom. Attachments, links to other resources or websites, videos on YouTube and Google Drive files can be attached by the teacher to the assignments. You can also gain extra means for having your assignment distributed to the students if these attached files are Google Docs, Google Sheets or Google Slides. Once you have clicked on the Google Docs, Google Sheets or Google Slides file, a drop- down menu is made visible which entails three options: Students can view file, Students can edit file and Make a copy for each student. The 'Make a copy for each student' option allows you to create extra copies for each student. Clicking on either of those options means you cannot undo the option or make changes to the assignment. You will have to delete the whole assignment if you have made a mistake and then start all over again.

Question: As a parent or guardian, can one sign up for the Google Classroom and have access to the Google Classroom; the engagements, communications, comment and other activities?

Answer: It is not possible to sign up to the Google Classroom as a parent or guardian. As a parent or guardian, be sure to have registered in the school as a parent or guardian for a student. The teacher or the domain administrator will then send an invitation to your email inviting you to the Google Classroom as a guardian (guardian email summaries) although this does not give you access to the classroom itself. All that the invitation does is to help you track your student's (ward's) progress in the classroom as you receive daily or weekly summaries of the activities of your ward in the class, classwork and if they have any work missing.

WHO IS JEREMY PAGES?

Jeremy Pages is a tech-savvy programmer with a flair for writing. After years of studying information technology, Jeremy understood the priceless value of getting the most out of technology in modern society. So, he decided to share his knowledge with the rest of the world. Jeremy knows that children are our future, so he cares that every child receives a proper education. He wrote his first manual to help teachers, as well as their students, make the most out of Google Classroom. Besides giving invaluable technical advice, Jeremy also included tips on how teachers and students can bond in a virtual setting. Besides the manual on Google Classroom, Jeremy plans to prepare a few others that will allow teachers and students to experience a brand new dimension of virtual and distance teaching. Also, his guides shine a light on the subject of education and the importance of pupil-teacher relationship.